THE BOOK OF
CONQUESTS
JIM FITZPATRICK

WRITTEN AND ILLUSTRATED BY JIM FITZPATRICK
EDITED BY PAT VINCENT

To my mother Lily O'Connor FitzPatrick

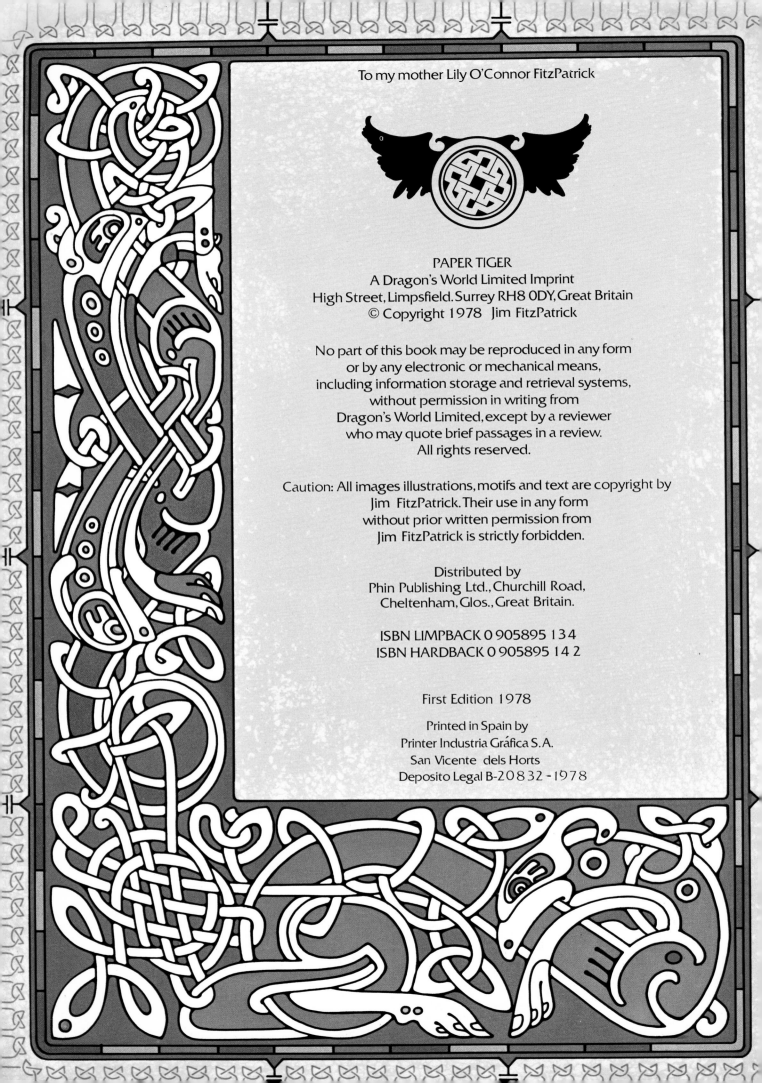

PAPER TIGER
A Dragon's World Limited Imprint
High Street, Limpsfield. Surrey RH8 0DY, Great Britain
© Copyright 1978 Jim FitzPatrick

Distributed by
Phin Publishing Ltd., Churchill Road,
Cheltenham, Glos., Great Britain.

ISBN LIMPBACK 0 905895 13 4
ISBN HARDBACK 0 905895 14 2

First Edition 1978

Printed in Spain by
Printer Industria Gráfica S.A.
San Vicente dels Horts
Deposito Legal B-20832-1978

CONTENTS

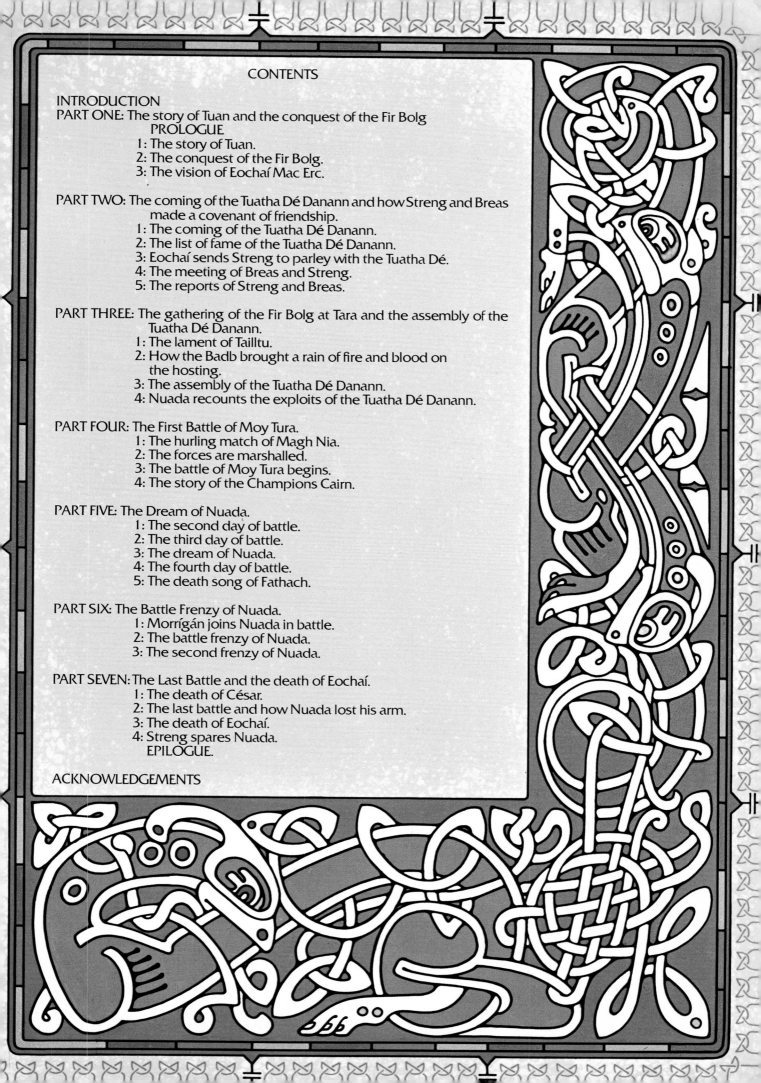

INTRODUCTION

The literature of ancient Ireland has been called 'the earliest voice from the dawn of western European civilisation'.

Unfortunately much of early Irish literature has been lost, what remains is contained in a few important manuscripts that have survived the centuries of warfare and invasion.

The earliest Irish stories are divided into four groups or cycles:

1) The Early Mythological Cycle.
2) The Ulster Cycle.
3) The Fenian Cycle.
4) The Historical Cycle.

The chief characters in the Early Mythological Cycle belong to the Tuatha Dé Danann (The Tribes of the Goddess Danu), a supposedly divine race which inhabited Éireann (Ireland) before the coming of the Celts.

The Ulster Cycle is composed of stories which tell mainly of the exploits of Cúchulainn, the Hound of Ulster; King Conchobor and the warriors of the Red Branch.

The Fenian Cycle is made up of the tales of the deeds of mighty Finn Mac Cumaill, his son Oisin, Conann Goll, Oscar and the champions of the Fianna.

The Historical Cycle contains stories of a more miscellaneous nature celebrating various high-kings of Ireland and set between the third century B.C. and the eighth century A.D.

The Book of Conquests is drawn from the Early Mythological Cycle and relates The Story of Tuan, The Coming of the Tuatha Dé Danann and The First Battle of Moy Tura.

Early story tellers working within the oral tradition found it difficult to determine whether the Tuatha Dé Danann were men, demons or gods.

The oldest of the surviving manuscripts is Lebor na h Uidre (The Book of the Dun Cow) written about the year 1100. This contains the story of Tuan which speculates about the origins of the Tuatha which,it says, even learned men did not know for certain though the wisdom and prowess of their race indicated a heavenly descent.

The heroic Tuatha Dé Danann are supposed to have fought and won two battles at Moy Tura. In the first battle they defeated the Fir Bolg and in the second they routed the Fomor.

According to T. F. O'Rahilly in his definitive work "Early Irish History and Mythology" the story of the first battle of Moy Tura was in existence before that of the second for which it served as a model. According to O'Rahilly the account of the battle was probably based on traditional stories accumulated around a historical fact: a great defeat suffered by the Fir Bolg in north-eastern Connacht.

O'Rahilly names the site of both battles as Moytirra (East and West), two adjoining townlands in the parish of Kilmactranny near Lough Arrow, County Sligo.

The father of Oscar Wilde, Sir William Wilde, conjectured that the site of the first battle was in the vicinity of Cong, County Galway,on account of the numerous cairns and primitive monuments still standing there. Indeed so certain was he of this that he had a home built for himself near Cong which he called 'Moytura House'!

The later Celtic invaders of Ireland worshipped the Tuatha Dé Danann as Gods and according to surviving manuscripts they continued to be honoured as divinities as late as the fifteenth century. In Lebor Gabála Éireann (The Book of the Taking of Ireland), known also as The Book of Invasions, the poet, probably a Christian scribe writing about 1100 A.D., finds it necessary to comment that 'though he enumerates them, he does not worship them.'

In early times, traditional tales such as The Story of Tuan, The Coming of the Tuatha Dé Danann and The First Battle of Moy Tura were transmitted and preserved from generation to generation by the several orders of druids. These sagas served as the oral 'scriptures' of the pre-Christian Celts of Ireland and blessings were said to accrue to those who related them accurately and to those who heard them told.

We cannot tell how changed these stories have been through their repeated tellings, but we have an indication that the greatest care was taken to ensure the integrity of the tradition. In the colophon to Táin Bó Cuailnge, the greatest of all the Irish sagas in the twelfth century Christian manuscript The Book of Leinster, it is written:

'A blessing on all who memorise the Tain with fidelity in this form and do not put any other form to it.'

However in a second colophon written in Latin (therefore more influenced by Christianity) we read a stern warning against taking the pagan contents too seriously:

'But I who have written this history, or rather story, do not give faith to many of the things in this history or story. For some things therein are delusions of the demons, some are poetic figments, some are truth, some are not, and some are for the amusement of fools.'

The ancient Celts were a cultured warrior-race with a rigidly structured social organisation. Their religion was administered by druids who jealously guarded their eloquent heritage of heroic legends and sagas.

Even today in Donegal, Cork, Kerry and the west of Ireland these tales and the ancient arts survive kept vividly alive by local storytellers and musicians.

It was in Clare that I, as a boy, first heard in fireside tellings the stories of the Shí or the Fairy Folk as the Tuatha Dé Danann are known today. In those legendary tales of my home countryside there was material enough for a dozen books of myth and folklore.

These stories have been passed on through generations by the tellers or 'seanchaí' as they are called in my native tongue but they always end in the traditional words:

'Now that's my story. If there's a word of a lie in it be it so! It was not I who invented it.'

Such respect for ancient tradition has made the west of Ireland and the Islands a deep lake of legend in which the hearer and the reader may catch glimpses of a long-vanished world, the dim and wavering outlines of a glorious age now passed.

Golden images of those past riches emerge in The Story of Tuan, The Coming of the Tuatha Dé Danann and The First Battle of Moy Tura, the three great stories that make up the first volume of The Book of Conquests.

In the cause of good story telling I have found it necessary to fill in obvious gaps in the original accounts and I have tried to do this as honestly as possible drawing on manuscript and other reliable sources (see page 110).

I have embellished the narrative where I felt it was necessary, reduced interminable lists of heroes and avoided much of the ritualistic repetition and convention which the modern reader, unused to the ways of oral tradition, might find tedious. I have used Tuan as the link, the resonant voice of myth and legend throughout and kept to the sequence of events described in The Story of Tuan and Lebor Gabála Éireann.

Occasionally to avoid confusion, I have merged two lesser characters into one and emphasised the roles of other, more important, characters such as Nuada, Streng and Éochaí.

"Gaelic-speaking Ireland" as W. B. Yeats pointed out in his Preface to Lady Gregory's 'Gods and Fighting Men', "because its art has been made, not only by the artist choosing his material from wherever he has a mind to, but by adding a little to something which has taken generations to invent, has always had a popular literature."

My material was forged for me long ago; I can only hope I have done it justice in the telling.

JIM FITZPATRICK 1978.

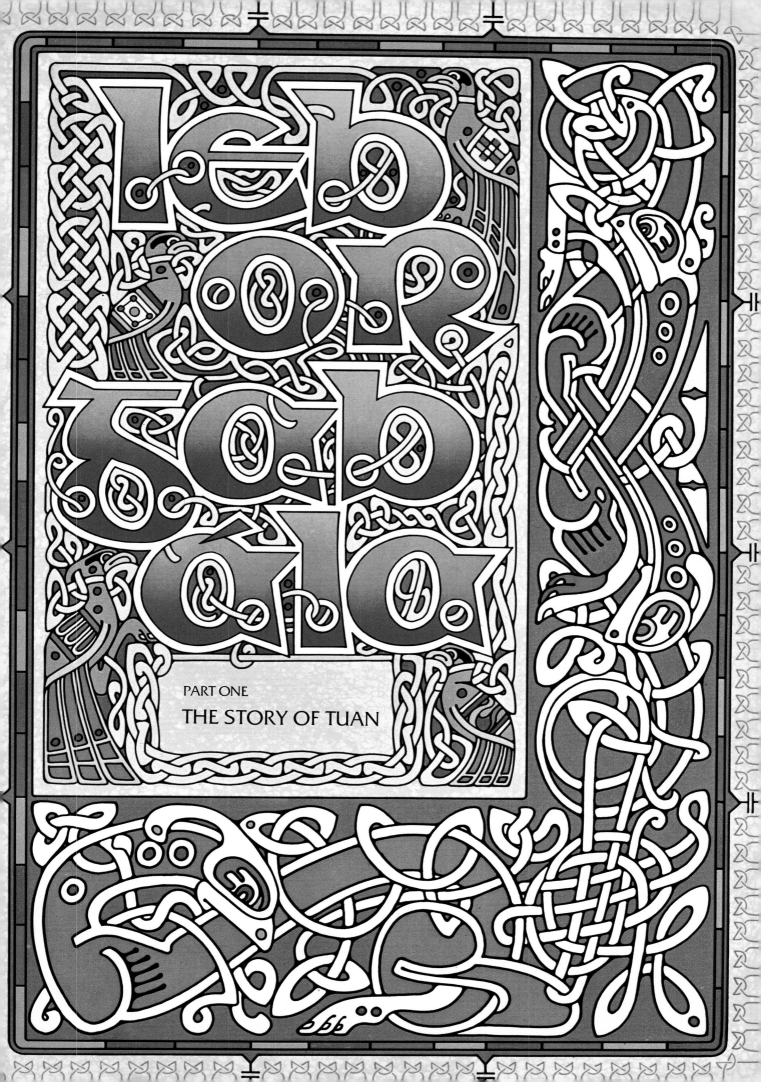

PART ONE

THE STORY OF TUAN

I am Tuan
I am legend
I am memory turned myth.

Mine is the voice that speaks the story. It cannot be told truly except by me, for it is I who have unlocked the words from the secret hoard of my heart and mind.

This is my story.

Born a child of the Golden Age
I spoke first the innocent words of men,
But to learn the secrets inscribed by Time
I hearkened to dark whispers of Ancient Craft.

I have lived through life in many forms.
I have been man and beast, sea and sky.
I have died and been reborn more often
Than I can truly remember.

I have witnessed what the wisest never imagined.
I have trodden ways beyond all dreaming of man.

I have lived through the Dark Age of the earth
When savagery and sorcery shadowed the land;
Great cities of gold tumbled beneath raging seas
And slumbering monsters rose from the deep.

All fair works perished.
The power of evil turned bright day
Into perpetual night.
The children of the earth
Were lost in darkness, threatened by death.

I, Tuan, once a king,
Hid in the shape of beast and bird
And locked the speech of man
In the fastness of my heart.

I am Tuan.
I am legend.
I am guardian of man's courage and his dreams.
By turf embers many tongues have spoke my tale,
But still I am keeper of this story:

The saga of The First Battle of Moy Tura and
The Conquest of the Tuatha Dé Danann.

JIM FITZPATRICK

1. THE STORY OF TUAN

I, Tuan, was once a man of wisdom and renown. I was the White Ancient, chieftain of the tribe of Cessair, first men to dwell in green and fertile Éireann.

I lived in peace until the Great Flood drowned my race leaving me the solitary companion of bird and beast, alone in a land grown strange and desolate.

For twenty-two years I, Tuan, now chieftain without tribe, dwelt in waste places and empty fortresses, seeking shelter from wolves and shunning the marauding bands of strangers that haunted shores once mine.

Then came Partholón and his people; strong men of sweet deeds and gentle ways. I dwelt in peace amongst them until a terrible pestilence destroyed them all. Once more I alone was left survivor, keeper of yet another tale, both blessed and cursed among men, Tuan, the White Ancient.

My strength left me and I became grey-haired, clawed, naked and miserable in my old age. My own shadow frightened me. Even the sound of a bird in flight or the creaking of a wind-blown bough made me cringe in my weakness.

The creatures of the forest scented my presence and knew I was alone. The long wolves haunted my dwelling-place: terrible shadows, silent and grey. They drove me from ruined fortresses to the forests, from from the forests to the cliffs.

There was no creature so weak it could not hunt me; there was no creature so timid it could not outface me. I learned to live as a beast forgetting all that I had known as a man. I could pad softly as any wolf; I could run tirelessly as the boar. Yet still deep in my heart I craved the company of men; voices calling my name, hands grasping mine.

One morning, gazing from the headland above my cave I saw another fleet approach this sheltered isle. My heart leapt for joy as the great prows rounded the land. I followed them along the wind-torn cliffs, springing from rock to rock like a wild cat.

Then as the ships swung in to anchor, I stopped to cool myself. Crouching over a pool to drink I saw myself mirrored in bright water.

I saw that I was hairy and naked; claws curved from my hands and feet. No sign of my manhood was left; I beheld myself brother of beasts not heroes.

I looked and I wept.

For on those faded sails I had seen the serpent and the rod, the

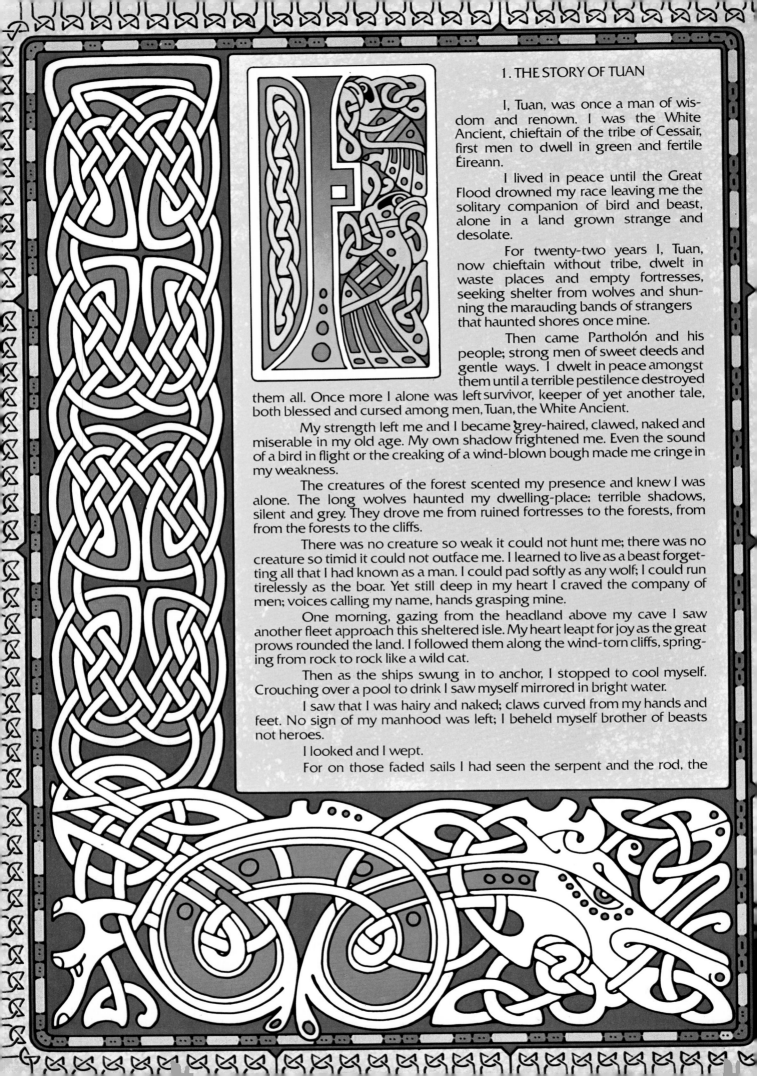

insignia of my father's race, yet now I did not dare approach them.

I hid in my cave and grief brimmed my heart. I could do no more than howl my lamentations to the earth and the sky. Only echoes answered my despair.

Then a great storm arose and the fleet pitched and tossed as if blown by a giant's breath. The waves raised the boats to the sky and wind caught them like the leaves of autumn and dashed them against the streaming rocks. The bowels of the ships were broken open by sharp stone and heavy water. The wind strode down from the heavens like a god carving a way through the banked storm clouds with forked spears of lightening and bolts of thunder.

The lonely shelter of my cave was welcome to me as I watched the longships scatter and break like matchwood spilling their treasure of men.

Above the clamour and tumult of the storm there came a pitiful sound, thin and distant as though from the ocean's depths; the sound of drowning men calling to their gods, crying for their loved ones.

Then a great sadness came upon me and the horror of that night weighed on me pressing me down into a black slumber.

I slept for many days, floating loose in dream-time. I saw my mortal form change from aged man to powerful beast: in my dreams I became a stag. Through the heaviness of sleep I felt the beat of a new heart, the strength of young sinews and limbs.

I awoke from my sleep
I became my dream
I, Tuan, was a stag.

I was young again and glad of heart. My limbs were freed from the curse of age and sickness. I leapt with wild strides; the air curled round me; the ground shook beneath me and the deer herd ran with me.

I raised my antlers to salute the rising sun and as the morning set fire to the snow-white clouds I sang of the coming of Nemed and of my own transformation:

I am Tuan.
I am legend.
I am the great-horned stag.
My skin is strong; rough and red;
I move easily across the land of Éireann.
From the headlands I turn to the rising sun
And sing of the coming of Nemed.

It was Nemed and his race who came to Éireann in that great fleet and of his thirty-four ships only nine escaped the storm and landed on our sacred isle.

But the time of Nemed was a time of suffering, for his people were sorely harassed by an alien race, the Fomor, dark-skinned barbarians born

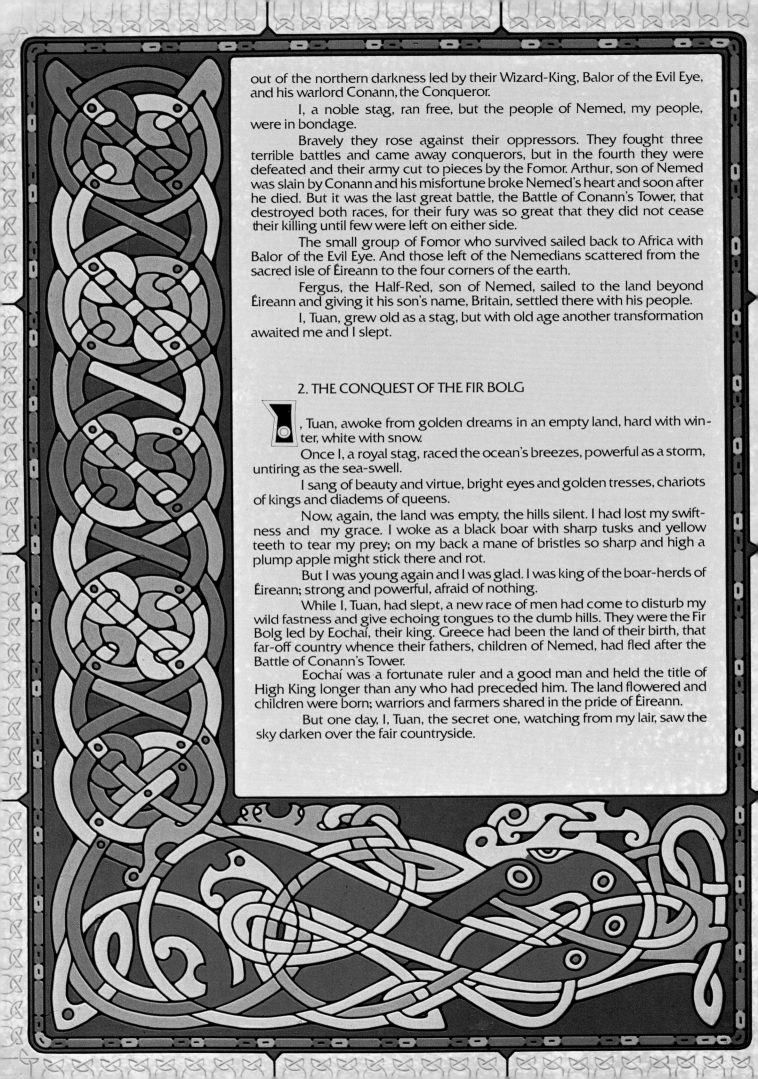

out of the northern darkness led by their Wizard-King, Balor of the Evil Eye, and his warlord Conann, the Conqueror.

I, a noble stag, ran free, but the people of Nemed, my people, were in bondage.

Bravely they rose against their oppressors. They fought three terrible battles and came away conquerors, but in the fourth they were defeated and their army cut to pieces by the Fomor. Arthur, son of Nemed was slain by Conann and his misfortune broke Nemed's heart and soon after he died. But it was the last great battle, the Battle of Conann's Tower, that destroyed both races, for their fury was so great that they did not cease their killing until few were left on either side.

The small group of Fomor who survived sailed back to Africa with Balor of the Evil Eye. And those left of the Nemedians scattered from the sacred isle of Éireann to the four corners of the earth.

Fergus, the Half-Red, son of Nemed, sailed to the land beyond Éireann and giving it his son's name, Britain, settled there with his people.

I, Tuan, grew old as a stag, but with old age another transformation awaited me and I slept.

2. THE CONQUEST OF THE FIR BOLG

I, Tuan, awoke from golden dreams in an empty land, hard with winter, white with snow.

Once I, a royal stag, raced the ocean's breezes, powerful as a storm, untiring as the sea-swell.

I sang of beauty and virtue, bright eyes and golden tresses, chariots of kings and diadems of queens.

Now, again, the land was empty, the hills silent. I had lost my swiftness and my grace. I woke as a black boar with sharp tusks and yellow teeth to tear my prey; on my back a mane of bristles so sharp and high a plump apple might stick there and rot.

But I was young again and I was glad. I was king of the boar-herds of Éireann; strong and powerful, afraid of nothing.

While I, Tuan, had slept, a new race of men had come to disturb my wild fastness and give echoing tongues to the dumb hills. They were the Fir Bolg led by Eochaí, their king. Greece had been the land of their birth, that far-off country whence their fathers, children of Nemed, had fled after the Battle of Conann's Tower.

Eochaí was a fortunate ruler and a good man and held the title of High King longer than any who had preceded him. The land flowered and children were born; warriors and farmers shared in the pride of Éireann.

But one day, I, Tuan, the secret one, watching from my lair, saw the sky darken over the fair countryside.

3. THE VISION OF EOCHAÍ MAC ERC

his was to be the last winter of Eochaí's reign.

King of Éireann, his days were troubled by rumours of a great fleet led by Balor of the Evil Eye, of black and green sails filling the Western seas casting their shadows before the setting sun. Father of his people, his sleep was broken by strange visions. His heart sad and anxious Eochaí called his wise man to him.

The wizard César came to his king. Eochaí spoke:

"In my dream I saw a great flock of black birds rising from the depths of the ocean. Covering our land they tore our soft flesh with sharp beaks and fought with our people. But one amongst us rose up and cut off a wing from the noblest of them.

"Even so I saw nightmare chasms choked with the bodies of the slain. The rivers ran red and the black birds settled on mountains of skulls and feasted horribly on carrion and broken bones, the bodies of our sons and brothers.

I have spoken my dream, César. Use your secret skills to unlock its meaning."

César did as he was asked, and by means of ritual and sorcery devined the vision of the King, making plain what had been concealed by veils of sleep.

"Sad words I bring you, O king. From across the sea warriors of the race of Nemed will come to Éireann. They will come, sailing the winds and the high air as the birds did, in a great fleet; a thousand heroes in speckled-sailed ships with raven-winged war witches presaging death.

Evil days will come to you, signs to lead you astray, for this is a race skilled in all the arts of sorcery. They will be victorious in every battle.

It was our bones the black birds fought over in your dream, for we will be the first slain and the pickings represent our tributes."

Great anguish filled the King's heart. His words were heavy and sorrowful.

"It is people of our own blood, sons of Nemed, who come to Éireann as our enemies. My dream has foretold the terrible slaughter of kinsmen."

And so it happened that César spelled out the dream of Eochaí that spoke of The Coming of the Tuatha Dé Danann and told of The First Battle of Moy Tura.

Lebor Gabála

PART TWO

THE COMING OF THE
TUATHA DÉ DANANN

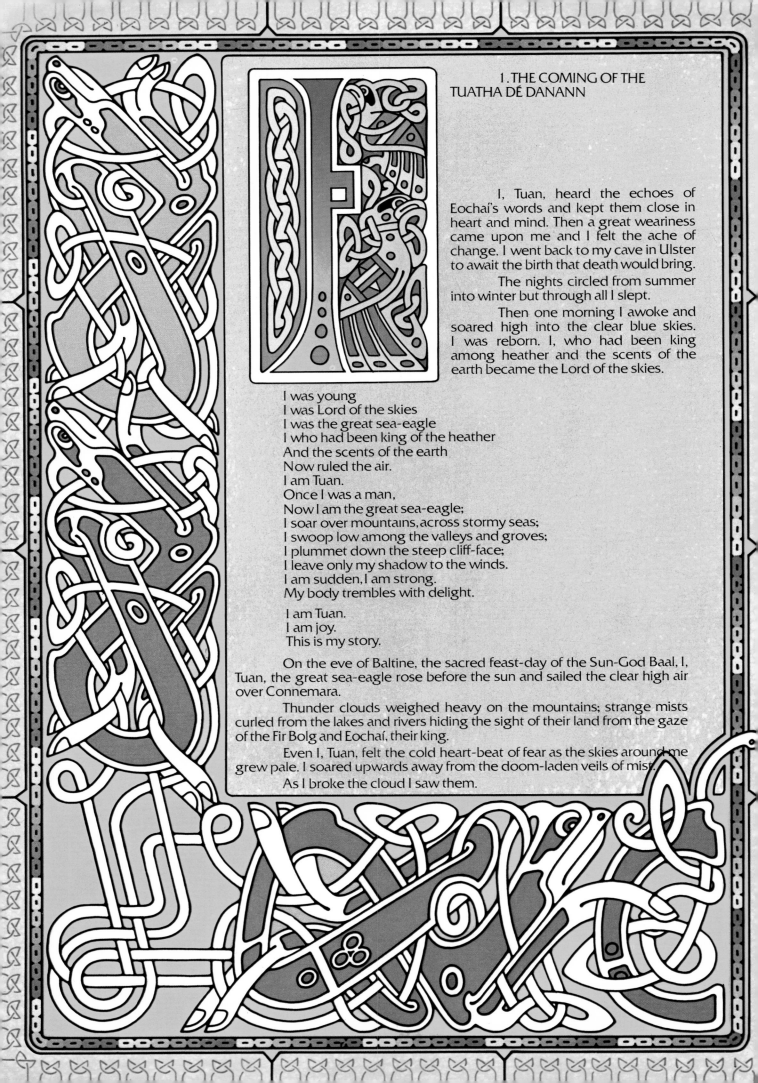

1. THE COMING OF THE TUATHA DÉ DANANN

I, Tuan, heard the echoes of Eochaí's words and kept them close in heart and mind. Then a great weariness came upon me and I felt the ache of change. I went back to my cave in Ulster to await the birth that death would bring.

The nights circled from summer into winter but through all I slept.

Then one morning I awoke and soared high into the clear blue skies. I was reborn. I, who had been king among heather and the scents of the earth became the Lord of the skies.

I was young
I was Lord of the skies
I was the great sea-eagle
I who had been king of the heather
And the scents of the earth
Now ruled the air.
I am Tuan.
Once I was a man,
Now I am the great sea-eagle;
I soar over mountains, across stormy seas;
I swoop low among the valleys and groves;
I plummet down the steep cliff-face;
I leave only my shadow to the winds.
I am sudden, I am strong.
My body trembles with delight.

I am Tuan.
I am joy.
This is my story.

On the eve of Baltine, the sacred feast-day of the Sun-God Baal, I, Tuan, the great sea-eagle rose before the sun and sailed the clear high air over Connemara.

Thunder clouds weighed heavy on the mountains; strange mists curled from the lakes and rivers hiding the sight of their land from the gaze of the Fir Bolg and Eochaí, their king.

Even I, Tuan, felt the cold heart-beat of fear as the skies around me grew pale. I soared upwards away from the doom-laden veils of mist.

As I broke the cloud I saw them.

Sailing the winds above the purple mountains of Connemara, and beyond through the high air and low air that rose and blew among the Red Hills of Rein, was a great fleet.

Shrouded by magic mists, borne on strong winds, the Tuatha Dé Danann came in their great mystical ships Raven-emblazoned sails at full stretch.

Beneath the sky of stars the truth is not known whether they were of the heaven or of the earth, sons of demons or of men.

I, Tuan, alone witnessed their coming.

On my curved wings I flew with the enchanted ships and I sang my song of greeting.

I invoke the name of Nemed,
The land of Éireann,
Our God the Sun.
I, Tuan, welcome you.
Welcome to the green mountains,

The dancing shadows of the woods,
The rippling bright waters,
The fish-filled lakes.
It is your land awaits you.

Now pride, not fear, pulsed in my heart keeping time with the drumbeat of the oars. Bright standards and silken banners coloured like all the flowers of the world flew from their mast-heads in the high air.

So I saw the coming of the long ships of the Tuatha Dé Danann into the valleys of Connacht. Each one was hung with magical shields and their sides painted with runes and oghams. The sun, hidden from the Fir Bolg, rose high to touch the armour of these painted strangers with fire and life. For the black-sailed ships did not come from the land of Death but were driven by the strength and magic skill of mortal men, heroes, the like of whom have not been seen in the land of Éireann before or since.

A thousand heroes and their followers came with that fleet to Éireann. At their head was a warrior king, a flame-haired giant who stood against the sun, his red, chequered cloak billowing in the restless wind. This was Nuada, King of the Tuatha Dé Danann.

I, Tuan, eagle and story bearer, flew with Nuada and his longships above the purple hills of Connemara and at last came to rest with them against the Red Hills of Conmaichne Reine in Connacht.

2. THE LIST OF FAME OF THE TUATHA DÉ DANANN

Nuada, King of the Tuatha Dé Danann, turned his keen pale eyes towards the green valleys of his ancestral homeland and gave thanks to his god, the Sun.

A giant among men, a hero among immortals, he stood against the rising sun. His flaming red hair was tipped with white, as was the custom of his race and crowned by the sacred battle helmet of the Tuatha Dé with its silver horns and engraven signs of rank and race.

Under a bodice of studded gold and bronze armour he wore a robe

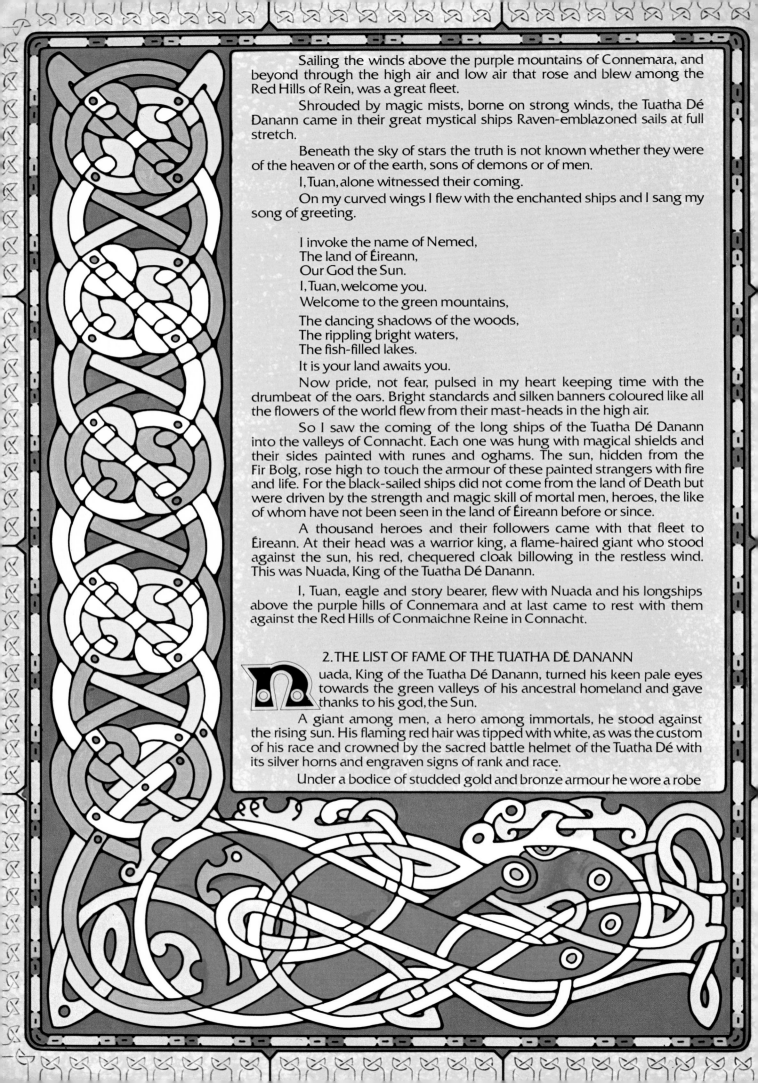

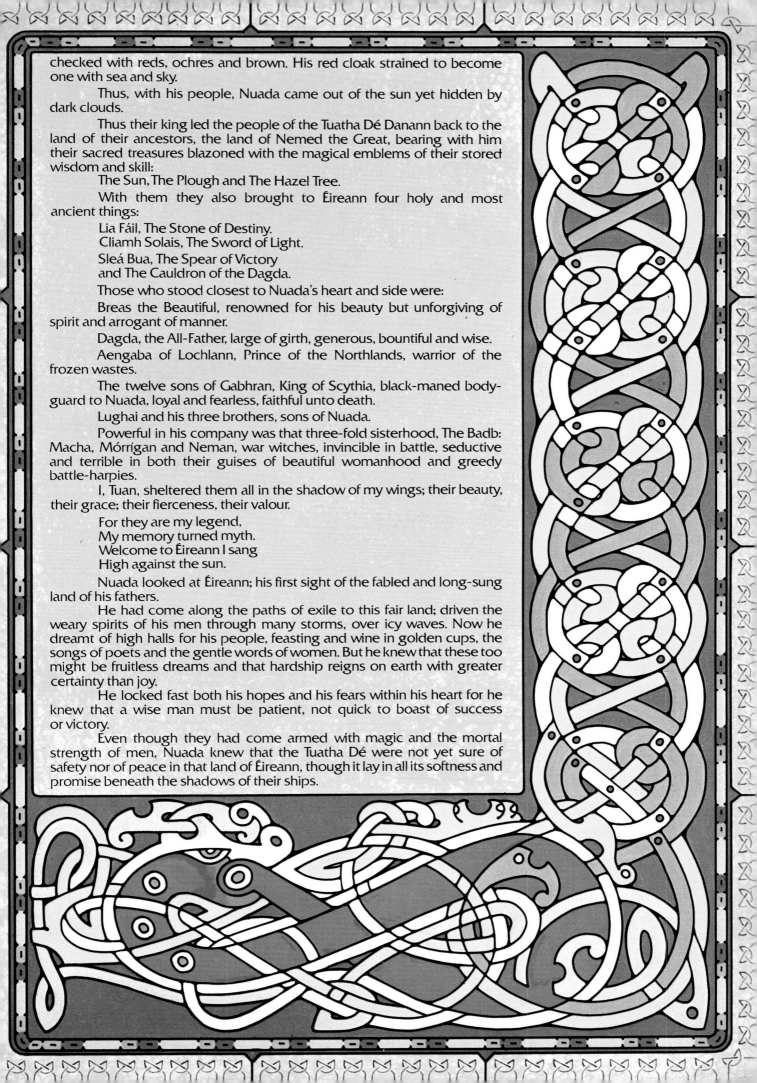

checked with reds, ochres and brown. His red cloak strained to become one with sea and sky.

Thus, with his people, Nuada came out of the sun yet hidden by dark clouds.

Thus their king led the people of the Tuatha Dé Danann back to the land of their ancestors, the land of Nemed the Great, bearing with him their sacred treasures blazoned with the magical emblems of their stored wisdom and skill:

The Sun, The Plough and The Hazel Tree.

With them they also brought to Éireann four holy and most ancient things:

Lia Fáil, The Stone of Destiny.
Cliamh Solais, The Sword of Light.
Sleá Bua, The Spear of Victory
and The Cauldron of the Dagda.

Those who stood closest to Nuada's heart and side were:

Breas the Beautiful, renowned for his beauty but unforgiving of spirit and arrogant of manner.

Dagda, the All-Father, large of girth, generous, bountiful and wise.

Aengaba of Lochlann, Prince of the Northlands, warrior of the frozen wastes.

The twelve sons of Gabhran, King of Scythia, black-maned body-guard to Nuada, loyal and fearless, faithful unto death.

Lughai and his three brothers, sons of Nuada.

Powerful in his company was that three-fold sisterhood, The Badb: Macha, Mórrígan and Neman, war witches, invincible in battle, seductive and terrible in both their guises of beautiful womanhood and greedy battle-harpies.

I, Tuan, sheltered them all in the shadow of my wings; their beauty, their grace; their fierceness, their valour.

For they are my legend,
My memory turned myth.
Welcome to Éireann I sang
High against the sun.

Nuada looked at Éireann; his first sight of the fabled and long-sung land of his fathers.

He had come along the paths of exile to this fair land; driven the weary spirits of his men through many storms, over icy waves. Now he dreamt of high halls for his people, feasting and wine in golden cups, the songs of poets and the gentle words of women. But he knew that these too might be fruitless dreams and that hardship reigns on earth with greater certainty than joy.

He locked fast both his hopes and his fears within his heart for he knew that a wise man must be patient, not quick to boast of success or victory.

Even though they had come armed with magic and the mortal strength of men, Nuada knew that the Tuatha Dé were not yet sure of safety nor of peace in that land of Éireann, though it lay in all its softness and promise beneath the shadows of their ships.

3. EOCHAÍ SENDS STRENG TO PARLEY WITH THE TUATHA DÉ

The Fir Bolg saw nothing of the coming of the Tuatha Dé Danann for the mist of their destiny lay heavy upon them and the lands around them.

Both kinsman and foe were hidden from them until report came of a great gathering fortified among the Red Hills of Rein, hemmed about by strong ramparts, sharp staves and pointed stones.

It was thus that Eochaí learned of the presence of the Tuatha Dé Danann and knew that the time of his vision was upon him.

Summoning his chieftains to Royal Tara, Eochaí addressed them:

"We do not know who these men are, neither their strength nor their intent.

You, Streng, our champion, set out for Connacht. You are bold to spy on hosts and challenge strangers. You are proud, powerful and terrifying to behold."

Streng rose slowly from the shadows of the great Hall of Hostings and, without a word, took down from the wall behind him, his bronze-rimmed and blazoned longshield; his two thick-shafted javelins; his bone-handled, death-dealing sword; his four-cornered bull-horned war-helmet; his finely-honed battleaxe; his iron war club and drew on his battleshirt of chain-link mail.

His fierce eyes burning, his flaxen hair streaming over his shoulders, Streng circled Royal Tara nine times. Then he bade farewell to his loved ones and went on his way to Conmaichne Rein in Connacht.

For many days Streng journeyed through the vast forests and oak woods of Éireann. He walked through the secret places known to him since childhood; along the path of fox and badger, dappled with hazel shadows, beside dark lakes and streams which caught the glimmer of stars and fed the flashing silver of the fish.

He slipped across stone-stepped rushing rivers through dew-laced fern-abounding fields. He raced the winds that danced across the lush green meadowlands of Royal Meath. Small beasts and birds lay invisible as he passed and the hawk was cheated of its prey. The rain, the wind, the sun of his native land slanted against the strength of his limbs and the tender fairness of his hair as he trod the shadows of the fleeting clouds.

At last he came to the place where the Tuatha Dé Danann had set their camp.

In the shelter of the forest's edge he set about painting his body with blue woad, white chalk and the juice of the red berry. He limed his blond hair and twisted it until it stood out stiff as a taut rope from the nape of his neck and sprang from beneath his helmet like a wild horse's mane.

Then Streng strode out from the thicket to meet the strangers, a painted giant striking terror in the hearts of those who kept watch over the hosts of the Tuatha Dé. Messengers ran with word of the strange warrior to Nuada their king.

"A huge man, painted for battle comes alone to our camp," they said. "He is well armed and has the bearing of a champion."

The king consulted with Dagda, the All-Father who was wisest of the elders of the Tuatha Dé Danann, and others of his most experienced warriors.

JIM FITZPATRICK

The Dagda spoke:

"Since he is alone he comes only to learn of our origins, whence and why we are here. Let us send Breas, our champion, to parley with the stranger. Better to find out his intent, than to rush hastily to challenge him."

Then Breas the Beautiful, son of Elathan the Immortal, went out from the camp to hear the stranger's words and to inspect his weapons as was the custom in those days. He was resolved not to demand battle but only to fight if the stranger struck him first.

4. THE MEETING OF BREAS AND STRENG

breas strode forth carrying with him his two great spears with their deadly thin points, his two-handled sword and his bronze-bossed shield. He wore his dragon-emblazoned helmet and his swirling ash-blond hair shone beneath the noonday sun.

Cautiously the two heroes approached each other; Streng resplendent in the panoply of war, Breas magnificent in the radiance of his beauty. Streng wondered at the great spears he saw and rested his speckled shield on the ground so that it protected his face and body.

Breas too kept his silence holding his shield before him.
In the high air between sea and mountain
I, Tuan, was unregarded witness of that meeting.
Two heroes, one a warrior, battle-scarred,
One a champion, blessed in beauty,
Met beside the rippling waters.

At last Breas spoke, the champion sent from the Tuatha Dé. He gave account of the coming of his people. When Streng heard that the fair stranger spoke his own tongue the knot of his heart and mind loosened and he replied freely:

"I greet you as a brother, for we are both of the race of Nemed. Remember this when you return and tell your king we share the same noble blood. Let neither pride nor greed shadow our friendship, nor cut down the flower of our race."

"Remove your shield," said Breas "so that I may see you and give my people a just account of your appearance."

"I will," said Streng. "It was only from fear of your thin-pointed spears that I placed my shield between us."

When Streng raised his shield Breas said.

"Strange and venomous are those thick-handled spears of yours. I would like to look at them."

So Streng unbound the leather tyings of his Craiseachs, as his heavy spears were called, and handed them to Breas who weighed them in his hands.

Then Breas spoke:

"I have not seen their like before; broad-pointed, near-blunt, stout and heavy, mighty and strong.

"Woe to him against whom they shall be cast.

"Death is in their strong blows; destruction in one thrust; deadly wounds in their hard plying."

"They are called Craiseachs" said Streng.

"Powerful weapons indeed," said Breas "they mean bruised and broken bodies, gaping wounds and crushed bones, broken shields and certain death.

"Let us settle this matter before the blood of our brothers stains the sacred soil of Éireann. Tell me who you are and where you come from."

Streng came over to Breas, standing next to him like a brother and told him the history of the Fir Bolg, of their leader Eochaí, who held the title Árd-Rí, High King of Éireann, and how their allies the Fir Domhnann and the Galeoin were all descended from the race of Nemed.

"We too are of the race of Nemed," said Breas. "We are the Tuatha Dé Danann; Nuada is our king. We came from the North in a cloud of mist and magic shower and sailed down from the heavens to the sacred isle of Éireann."

Streng did not believe it was thus but he held his peace and said only:

"I have a long journey and must go. Give me your terms to settle this affair."

"Go then," said Breas "Here is one of the two sharp javelins I brought with me. We call them Sleghs. Take this and show your people against what weapons they will have to fight."

In exchange Streng handed Breas one of his heavy handled Craiseachs, for him to show in turn to the Tuathe Dé.

"Tell the Fir Bolg," said Breas, "that they must give our people half of Éireann or face us in battle."

"For myself," answered Streng, "I would rather give you half of Éireann than face your deadly weapons. But it is not mine to give, so I must return to Eochaí, my king, at Royal Tara and give the assembly report of your words. Farewell brave warrior. We met in mistrust; we part in peace. From this day we are bound as brothers."

Thus did Streng and Breas return each to their own people after pledging brotherhood and friendship.

I, Tuan, circling on curved wing high above the two heroes, remembered the dream of Eochaí and the fearful feasting of the black birds.

The past and the future were reflected in the unblinking circles of my eyes.   And I knew the days of peace in Eireann were numbered.

5. THE REPORTS OF STRENG AND BREAS.

For several days and nights Streng journeyed back through forests and oak-woods, meadows and heathland, until at last he reached the Hill of Tara and stood before his king Eochaí, and all the assembled chieftains of the Fir Bolg. Without pause he spoke:

"Theirs is a miraculous host; hostile and havoc-wrecking their heroes; sturdy and strong their shields; sharp and shaft-hard their spears; broad and bloody their blades. They will be fierce and terrible to fight. It would be wiser to make a fair division of the island and to give them

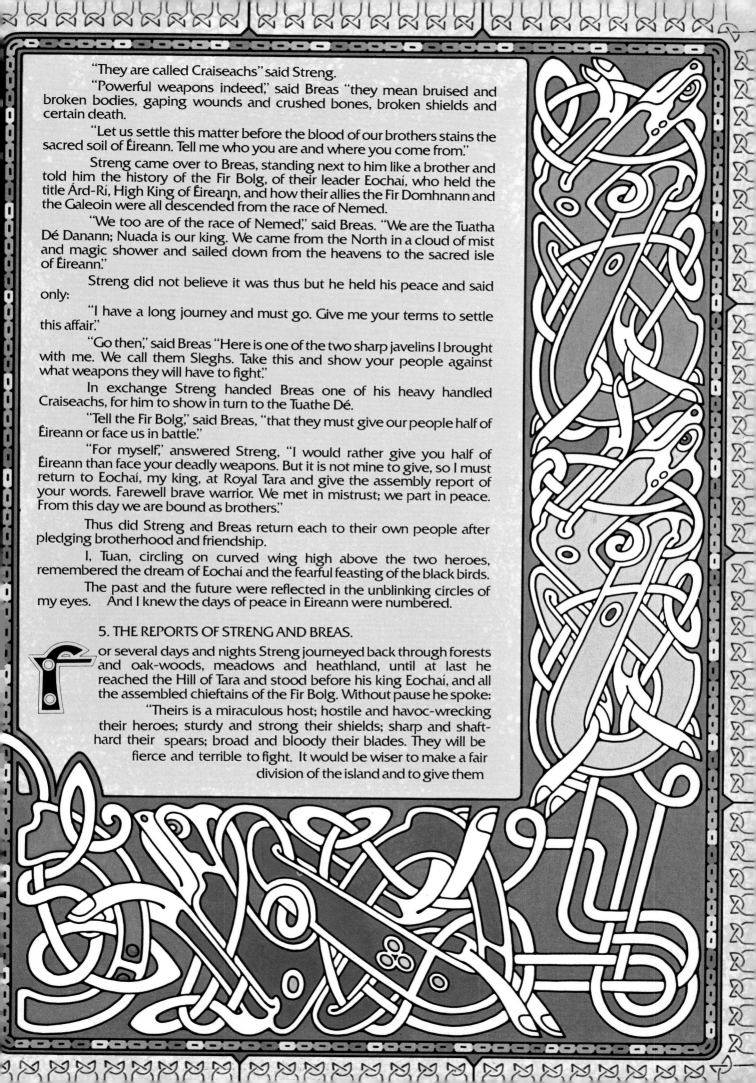

half as they wish, for they are of our own blood and the land is as sacred and hallowed to them as it is to us."

But the assembly did not go with Streng's advice or heed his wise counsel.

"Indeed we will not grant that demand," said the Fir Bolg; "For if we do, the land will be theirs for the taking in the end."

Then I, Tuan, spread my wings and rested on the winds over the camp of the Dé Danann and heard the words Breas spoke:

"He was a fierce and powerful man," said Breas, "moody and truculent, but tough and tenanious for all that, without fear of anyone of this earth. He gave me this heavy javelin so that you might know how the Fir Bolg deal out death and festering wounds to those who engage in battle with them."

When they heard these words the council of the Tuatha Dé Danann conferred together. At last the king, Nuada, spoke:

"We are not safe here. We will move to the western shore and there make a battle camp so well defended that we might face any who come, even be they sons of war-gods."

So the Tuatha Dé Danann travelled westward over the plains of Connacht, through forests and woodlands, over hills and across rocky wastelands, until they reached the fertile plain of Magh Nia.

There they fixed their camp and entrenched themselves at the westerly end of the plain with the fastness of the Black Hill, the great mountain Belgatan, behind them.

When they had fortified their camp all the chieftains of the Tuatha Dé gathered together and spoke thus:

"Strong and impregnable are our earthworks; unassailable are our ramparts. From here we will plan our battles and our hostings. From here we will wage our wars."

For long afterwards they sang this song in commemoration of that fateful day.

We hide in the shadow of the Black Hill;
We rest against the broad flanks of Belgatan.
From his high mountain we will go forth
To make wars against our enemy, raids on our foes.
Our will is strong; fearless we face the yet unknown,
In fierceness like the wolf, subtle as the mountain cat;
In cunning like the fox, swift-footed as the deer;
In splendour like the sun, violent as the thunder;
In strength like the rock, insistent as the sea.
We burn our silver ships, denying all retreat.
Earth-shaking warriors we stand by Belgatan
Ready to unloose the knots
That bind the spirit to the flesh.

I, Tuan, flew a high descant to the hymn of heroes.

LEBOR GABALA

PART THREE

THE GATHERING OF
THE FIR BOLG AT TARA

1. THE LAMENT OF TAILLTU.

When Eochaí, High King of Éireann and war-lord of the Fir Bolg, the Fir Domhnann, the Galeoin and the people of Cú Roi, heard that the Tuatha Dé Danann had fortified themselves at Belgatan he was dismayed.

"We must gather our forces," said Eochaí, "and prepare to fight for the holy ground of Éireann. Let messengers be sent to the five provinces so that we may assemble a strong army to march on the plain of Magh Nia."

Throughout the days that followed wave after wave of warriors descended on Royal Tara, seat of the High-King, and made their camps around the Hill of Hostings. From Connacht came the Fir Domhnann and Ga leoin; from Mumha came Rua the Bloody and the sons of Miled; from Ulster the people of Cú Roi, from Laighin the Fir Bolg led by their champion Streng and from the king's province, Royal Meath, came the army of Sláine the Fair, son of King Eochaí.

From the wilds of Ulster to the pasturelands of Mumha they came to Tara and gathered for the hosting; the peoples of the Fir Bolg meeting for the first time since the days of their fathers. The murmuring of many warriors rose to a mighty tumult just as the swelling sea finally thunders against the western coastlands. Like the flocks of countless birds that gather in the Meadows by the Blackwater river the heroes swarmed around Royal Tara.

Tailltu, queen of the Fir Bolg stood before the Royal Palace of Tara and tears filled her eyes as she watched the hosting in all its beauty and bravery. Standing apart she spoke an elegy for heroes:

"My words are lost like shadows in the host

JIM FITZPATRICK

My tears fall unnoticed with the dew
But may the gods hear my lone lament
Battle-hymn in cradle-song.

This day Death reaps bright harvest-time
But women will raise empty arms
And wail for husband, lover, son
And try to call their lost ones back.

My King goes forth to meet his fate
But I must stand aside and weep
And turn away my sorrowing face
And let the host go marching by."

2. HOW THE BADB BROUGHT A RAIN OF FIRE AND BLOOD ON THE HOSTINGS.

It was then, after the Tuatha Dé Danann had fortified themselves at Belgatan, that the Badb, those three fearsome war-witches, Macha, Mórrigan and Nemain went to Royal Tara where the tribes of the Fir Bolg were massing.

By the power of their magic they made the skies to close and darken over the Hill of Hostings. The birds of the air and the beasts of the field sought out their hiding places and fell still and silent.

I, Tuan, flew alone through the unnatural night.

Then, most terrible of all, the great standing-stones set around the plain began to sing. And their song grew louder until at last it conjured up the anguished scream of the Banshee that called on the lost souls of the damned to come to magnify the evil sorcery of the three-fold Badb.

Huge misshapen spectres stalked the sky that day and shadows of winged warriors, drenched in blood, fought in the thunder-rent heavens.

Rank after glittering rank of spearmen marched in endless procession towards certain death; lean and sinewy creatures gnawed at the flesh of corpses. Over all this unnatural feasting the Horned God Carnún presided in the guise of a terrible scaly-skinned dragon his red eyes glowing within the shadow of his body's huge serpentine folds.

I, Tuan, blown like a leaf on the winds of evil enchantment, heard the terror which burst from the hearts and lips of the Fir Bolg and saw the darkness of fear and foreboding that fell upon their camp.

The women and children wailed and cried. Even proud warriors and fearless heroes paled at the unnatural sights and hideous sounds that filled that black noon-tide.

Before the wide terror of their eyes the shadow of the Horned-Dragon God turned into a sanguine mist and a rain of blood and fire poured down from the torn heavens staining their flaxen locks and branding the

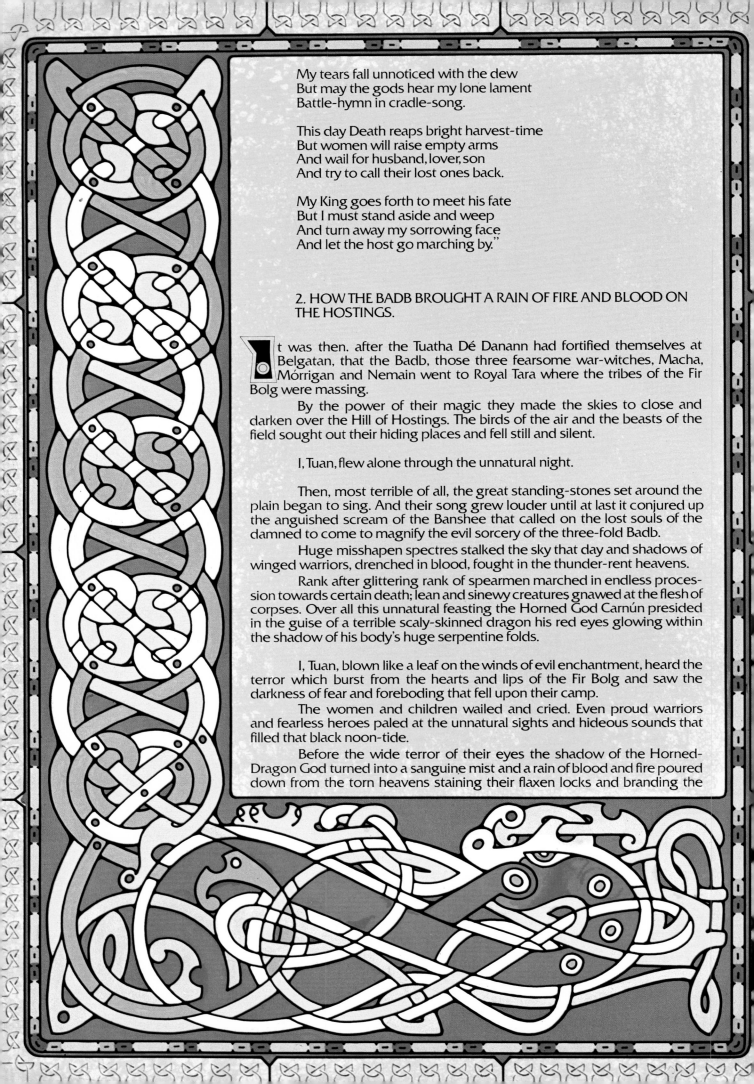

fairness of their skin.

The Fir Bolg beat their breasts in anguish and called in their despair on ancient gods, long since denied, to aid them against such powerful magic.

"Alas," they cried, "It is a terrible fate that the spells of our sorcerers cannot protect us against the witchcraft of the Tuatha Dé."

A great shaft of lightning split the heavens as César, wizard of Eochaí, king of the Fir Bolg, stepped before the great stone of Tara.

He called to Crom-Crúach, the elder god of his race, but his cry went unheard, drowned in the shrieking of the Banshé.

For three days César laboured to protect his people against the triple war-goddess and for three days the host of the Fir Bolg lay under the deadly cloud of rolling thunder and spectral shadows.

The red rain fell and the stench of death filled the air but still César called to his gods. He invoked the nine forms of Uath Mac Immomuin to intercede on his behalf with the Beast-God Baal. He wove his spells into the wind, the water, the earth and made a fine web of witchery to thwart the power of the Badb.

It was the night of the third day when César called once more to his elder god, the forbidden one, Crom-Crúach.

In a circle of limed grass he stood surrounded by hieroclyphs, runes and oghams burned out of the turf of the Hill of Hostings and coloured with white chalks, woad -blue and goat's blood.

No spectres dared enter this circle; no wind blew there, no blood-rain fell. This was a magic circle inscribed by sorcery, witchcraft and the blasphemous skills of César, wizard-prince and druid of the Fir Bolg tribes.

Slowly, ever more slowly, César had laboured to win a space of safety from sorcery of the Badb wherein his tormented people might rest in peace. But the three-fold witchcraft of the Badb was so powerful that even the awesome enchantments of the great César were as a handful of chaff flung against the east wind.

He knew that his gods had failed him. Now only his own secret powers stood against the overwhelming strength of the dreaded Badb.

He raised his open hands to the demon-shadowed skies and closed his ears to the shrieking of the stones.

"Crom-Crúach. Crom-Crúach!" he cried to the heavens, then lowered his head and chanted:

"Great creature from before the Flood,
Without sinew, without bone,
Without head, without feet,
Without flesh, without blood,
Great creature from beyond the stars,
Older than the race of man,
I, César of the Fir Bolg,

JIM FITZPATRICK

I call on you, O Great One,
You whose wisdom shaped the earth."

Nine times he chanted his invocation, each time lighting one of the long wax tapers set in a circle round the hill where Eochaí and the nobles of the Fir Bolg waited. As he lit the ninth and last taper, the flames flickered, then dimmed, until only the fine black traces of their smoke inscribed sinuous arabesques across the demon-haunted skies.

A great hush spread across the plain; the people of the Fir Bolg fell silent as the blood-rain ceased to fall and the shrieking of the stones turned to an anguished wail, drifting across the plain like a lost wind moaning among storm-bowed trees.

As the wailing died away a green light rose above the hosting of the Fir Bolg. It burned with an eerie intensity, lending strange life and form to the wavering columns of taper-smoke.

Once more César called on Crom-Crúach, speaking in the long-dead tongue of his forefathers and at the same time inscribed a magic symbol out of the black smoke with a thin silver dagger.

High above them the green fire grew so bright that it dazzled the assembled tribes and no man could ever say for certain what he saw that day.

But, I, Tuan, hung motionless on curved wing above the Hill of Tara that night, and I, Tuan, witnessed what men dared not describe.

The green fire formed an orb of blinding brightness as César sang his obscene invocations, his lips drawn tight against his teeth, like the snarl of a wild beast. As the green sphere spun and swirled a nightmare-demon reared up from its seething depths: Crom-Cruach, the Great Worm of myth and legend, writhed out of the drifting darkness of the smoke.

Again the standing stones of Tara began to moan and then howl as the very earth cried out in horror against the devil-ridden enchantment which deformed the very elements of nature. Then the spectres and shadows conjured up by the Badb quit the skies of Royal Tara with a great rush of spirit-wind; the voices of the stones were stilled and the enchantments of the fearful Badb were broken by César after three days and nights of terror and dismay.

I, Tuan, the Immortal Ancient, the great eagle, slept peacefully in my mountain eyrie that night, but the Elder Gods do not intervene in the affairs of man without price or purpose and I, Tuan, knew that the Fir Bolg and César their great wizard had a heavy debt to pay.

Though it was a dark and fearful time for the Fir Bolg they took heart from the success of their wizard and gathered their armies for an attack on the enemy camp.

When the warriors of the Fir Bolg were joined with those of the Galeoin, the Fir Domhnann and the people of Cú Roi, Laighin and Connacht they numbered eleven battle-hosts under the leadership of Eochaí, the

High King. After they had provisioned the army they marched westwards across the island to the plain of Magh Nia.

At their head was Eochaí,
With him   Streng his champion
and Sláine his son.
Behind came
Fathach, the poet,
César and his druids,
Rua the Bloody and the sons of Miled
And after them the Fir Bolg host.

3. THE ASSEMBLY OF THE TUATHA DÉ DANANN.

The sun was setting in golden splendour behind the Black Hill of Belgatan and from the great lakes pearly mists were rising, spilling out across the plain of Magh Nia, softening the brightness of the green grass and purple heather.

For two days I, Tuan, the sea eagle, had fished the seas beyond the Moher cliffs. Now I returned to watch the making of both battle and story on the plains below.

Out of the reddening skies I flew, over the darkening lowlands. I saw the armies of the Fir Bolg drawn up at the entrance of the plain, while at the western end the forces of the Tuatha Dé Danann were encamped against the great mountain Belgatan which the setting sun had crowned with its dying glory. But even as I flew towards it the darkness of night swallowed all light and only the distant thunder growled and murmured.

The Tuatha Dé lit a great fire against the threat of alien night; enormous shadows danced around the earthworks which circled the foot of Belgatan.

Nuada, the king, stared into the flames and saw visions there of the slaughter to come, the deaths of many brave warriors; the terrible price to be paid for the land of his forefathers.

He had been to Cnoc Nemed, the Sacred Mountain of Nemed and thus had fulfilled his Geassa, or bond, which he had promised at the time of his warrior-training with Scathach, the war-goddess of Scythia. He had led his people, the race of Nemed back to Éireann; he had spoken with the spirits of his ancestors, he had prayed to his gods. But now, though he had honoured his bond, was not the time for peace and celebration for the hour of his final and most grievous testing was at hand.

Behind him sat the assembly of the Tuatha Dé Danann gathered in silence around the orange glow. Death, they knew, also sat with them waiting to claim the price they would have to pay for the winning of their homeland.

I, Tuan, knew their pride and their pain.
I too had wandered homeless far from kin

JIM FITZPATRICK

Mindful of past glories; ruined halls;
Moss grown fortresses; fallen heroes.
When the people of Parthalon gathered in council
My words were heard and my advice sought.
The life and death of many warriors
Had been held in the balance of my word
As chieftain of my race, it was my hard fate
To deliver loved ones, in the flower of youth
To the pain of battle and to certain death.
Now a weighty secret and unspoken sadness
Filled the heart of Nuada as he, too,
Faced his day of destiny.

4. NUADA RECOUNTS THE EXPLOITS OF THE TUATHA DÉ DANANN.

At last Nuada turned his gaze to his warriors and spoke:

"Better to fight and die here than live for ever in the far-away lands of frozen Lochlann, or to be persecuted and taxed in Scythia. Better to be warrior and freeman in the green land of Éireann than to be slaves without rank or right in strange countries.

"Children of Nemed, hear me; it is your own story that I tell.

"I have been to the Sacred Mountain; I have spoken with our ancestors; I have prayed to our Gods. The Gods have put us to a thousand tests and we have faced them all with courage and with skill. We have stormed cities in Scythia and plundered the lands of the Philistines, and though we were often outnumbered, we triumphed by divine will and the strength of our arms.

"We have fought great fleets on the seas, vast armies on land. The Gods of the sea have sent violent storms against our ships. We have weathered them. The winds have taken us where they would, but could not destroy us. We have overthrown empires and brought ruin to our enemies.

"The Assyrians, whose forces out number all the races of these western Isles, defeated our allies the Athenians. Though we could never destroy such vast hordes, we fought them to a standstill and cut a bloody path through their ranks on our way to Scythia. A long, bitter journey it was too. Many gave their lives in that heroic march northwards but always we were victorious.

"We of the race of Nemed wandered the plains of Scythia for many years and fought many battles, until at last, we were driven from that land by cruel levies and harsh taxes. Among the many tribes of Scythia we found not only enemies, but friends as well and with these allies we grew strong and adventurous once more. When we moved across Cimmeria and Hyperborea to the frozen northlands of Lochlann they came with us. For seven years we stayed in those dark and icy lands of the North Wind and we taught the noble Northmen much of our learning, magic, and skills in warfare. Yet still we could not forget our native land of Éireann with its

dancing streams, the bird-song in the hazel groves, the gentle mists and warm rains.

"We survived those years of suffering and hardship, sustained by the visions of our seers and druids, the hopes of our peoples, the prophecies of our return to this our own, our native land.

"Therefore when the greater armies of the Fir Bolg approach do not despair, throw your fears across the plains with your javelins; for we have travelled many years, through many lands to see this day. With our victory this island will belong to us and be the home of our children and the race of Nemed."

These words of Nuada, their king, touched the hearts of the heroes of the Tuatha Dé Danann and as with one voice a great warcry burst from them and echoed against the dark flank of Belgatan.

I, Tuan, high in my mountain lair, heard that warcry, and shared the exultation of the heroes of the Tuatha Dé.

Then Breas, the greatest hero of the Tuatha Dé Danann, rose to his feet and offered his advice:

"Let us mix our courage with guile and sorcery so that victory will surely be ours.

"Let the Badb visit the Fir Bolg camp each night and distract their champions with the beauty of their bodies and the magic of seductive spells.

"Let Dian-cecht, our physician, prepare a well of healing; let the Druids prepare their spells.

"Let our war-smiths and craftsmen prepare for weapon-making and mending.

"Group your warriors and chieftains into tribes and clans. Thus each man will fight by his brothers side and never desert him, no matter how hard the fighting goes. Each battle-line will support the other and fight in turn so that our front will never be broken.

"Let each man follow the order of his commander, be he warrior, noble, or chieftain, for each has the cunning of a cat and the courage of a mountain lion. No man must lay down his life without glory or allow himself to be captured or ransomed; for he who obeys and fights according to our strategy need not be fearful of capture and humiliation.

"Now prepare yourselves for war. Paint your bodies, sharpen your javelins, hone your swords, adjust your shields and tyings, bind your clubs and axes.

"See that everything is ready for action and when it is, then above all be patient, for we will be slow to engage the enemy at first, rather we will try to mislead, delay and confuse the Fir Bolg, while encouraging them to divide and disperse their awesome armies.

"Take up your shields and the full burden of your fate, and set your mind on gallant deeds and certain victory, for the fight, when it comes will be a long, hard and bloody one."

The glowing embers of the fire broke and sent up a rush of flame

so that Breas stood illuminated in all his warlike splendour, like some young warrior-god stepped out of the shadows of perpetual night.

It was at that assembly that Nuada decided that envoys should be sent to the Fir Bolg camp in one final bid to avoid confrontation and certain slaughter.

Cairbre, Ai and Édan, the druids of the Tuatha Dé were selected as envoys and went to the tent of Eochaí, king of the Fir Bolg.

"We are here" they told Eochaí "to request the division of the land between us; the just partition of Éireann between all the children of the race of Nemed."

"Do the nobles of the Fir Bolg hear that?" said Eochaí.

"We do," they replied. "But the Tuatha Dé Danann may wait till Doomsday before their request be granted."

And so the die was cast for the great battle of Magh Nia, later called The First Battle of Moytura.

I, Tuan, folded my wings and rested awhile, for the custom of those ancient days was that each army should prepare weapons for the other side so that the valour of men and heroes might be seen more easily than the skill and wizardry of craftsmen.

The envoys of the Tuatha Dé were then given hospitality till this was arranged, and an armistice agreed until all weapons and equipment were ready, and the battle-lines were drawn.

The druids went back and reported the words of the Fir Bolg to Nuada and the Dé Dananns, and related how they had delayed the day of battle to frustrate the enemy, but the news that the Fir Bolg would not share the land with them and had refused favour and friendship caused them great distress.

"This is indeed" said Breas sadly "a day for lamentation, for those fierce fair-haired warriors are of our own flesh and blood."

Lebor Gabala

PART FOUR

THE FIRST BATTLE OF
MOY TURA

1. THE HURLING MATCH OF MAGH NIA.

With the battle delayed, the impatient hearts of the young warriors could not bear the tedium of waiting for the weapons to be prepared so Rua the Bloody and the twenty-seven sons of the tribe of Miled, allies of the Fir Bolg of Muma, sped westwards to the end of Magh Nia to challenge the Tuatha Dé to a hurling contest.

The youth of the Tuatha Dé were eager to meet them at the hurling which was a strong and skilful game. But they were no match for Rua and his tough mountain men. They had scored but one cúl when the wrath of the Fir Bolg descended on them like a tidal wave.

The skill and speed of the Dé Danann team could not match the brute strength and resolute savagery of Rua and his men; many bones were broken and youthful flesh bruised and gashed. The Tuatha Dé soon lost the game and Rua and his team left behind them the flower of the young hurlers of the Tuatha Dé Danann lying dead or grievously injured on the field.

It was a match that left great bitterness in the hearts of the Tuatha Dé Danann against Rua and the sons of Miled, allies of the Fir Bolg. From that day on they resolved to have their revenge upon them on the battle-field of Magh Nia.

The Cairn of the Match is the name of the cairn where they met, and Glen Cairn Aillem is the place where the dead are buried.

I, Tuan, saw that match from my eyrie high on Belgatan and I

shared the grief of the women of the Tuatha Dé for the loss of their finest sons and hurlers and for the humiliation they had to bear.

But Eochaí, High-King of the Fir Bolg was greatly heartened by this victory and called Fathach, his poet, to him and said:

"Go to the west and enquire of the nobles of the Tuatha Dé Danann how the battle is to be tomorrow, whether it is to be for one day's fighting or several."

Fathach went to the Dé Danann camp and after receiving their hospitality, put the question to Nuada, the Dagda, and Breas.

"What we have decided" they replied after conferring "is equal combat, with equal numbers on each side."

Now Eochaí was greatly distressed when he heard this because he knew the advantage lay with the Fir Bolg and their superior numbers. But since it was the decreed custom to allow the challenger his choice of weapon and mode of combat he knew he must abide by the decision of the Tuatha Dé Danann.

"Let us call Nert Chu, our strategist," said Eochaí "and follow his counsel, for he is wise and well-learned in the ways of war."

On the advice of Nert Chu the Fir Bolg raised a great fort and made a Well of Healing to close and heal the wounds of their warriors, and filled it with herbs.

The fort was later known as the Fort of the Blood-pools, from the pools of gore that surrounded the wounded, the dying and the dead.

When these earthworks were complete, their weapons ready, and their strategies devised, the Fir Bolg sent word to the Tuatha Dé that they were ready for battle.

The pattern of tomorrow's battle is yours," they told the Dé Danann, "What are to be your movements?"

"We will meet in the centre of the plain of Megh Nia with four battalions each," replied the Tuatha Dé Danann.

2. THE FORCES ARE MARSHALLED.

t was Midsummer's Day and the hosts rose with the first glimmer of sunlight. Brave warriors raised up their beautifully wrought and painted shields, and tied their hard-wood spears and heavy javelins to their right hands with leather thongs.

As the sun rose its golden light ran down to grooves of swords and spelt out their engraven charms in runes of fire.

Shoulder to shoulder, painted and adorned for battle the Fir Bolg followed their chieftains towards Magh Nia to meet their enemy.

Fathach, the Fir Bolg poet, stepped out from the tight ranks to encourage the fury of the advancing battalions and raise their spirits. His multicoloured tasselled cloak billowed in the east wind; his face was pale and his grey hair and beard were limed white at the tips, so that he looked like the god of time and passing seasons. In the midst of the great plain he had set up a great pillar of stone and now, standing by it, he raised his staff to the passing host, praising their valours, reminding them of past victories, and exhorting them to yet greater deeds of bravery in the coming conflict. Then as the glittering armies passed by him he could not restrain his tears of anguish and he cried out in his sadness:

"With what noble ceremony they advance. They go to gather up their fearless might on the plain of Magh Nia. But the army of the Tuatha Dé advance against the finely wrought swords of my brothers.

"The Badb, thirsty for blood, brood over the field of battle and many will be the gashed and mangled bodies where now the Fir Bolg stand in their pride.

"Tomorrow those who survive will weep to see the severed heads of their companions, brothers, sons and fathers, displayed with pomp and pride as battle trophies.

"Long after this battle is lost or won, pillars will stand to commemorate the victories of champions, the death of heroes. Where now the tall grass grows, a hundred pillars will soon stand and Magh Nia will be remembered as Moy Tura, the Plain of Pillars."

Against the Fir Bolg stood the army of the Tuatha Dé Danann, a solid wall of stout shields and deadly weapons. The sun danced on their bronze trappings making them as bright and beautiful as jewels strung out across the plain. They were as many as the speckled wild birds that haunt the oak-forests, as countless as the blossoms on the mountain heather.

I, Tuan, saw them thus for the last time in the fullness of their pride, their beauty and their youth, like jewels, like wild birds, like flowers. But their hearts beat high with rage and thoughts of slaughter and they were as restless as the flies that swarm the meadows at pasture-time.

Nuada and his Scythian bodyguard strode before his combat lines, their horsehair plumes floating on the drifting winds. But the privilege of leading the heroes into battle that day belonged to Dagda, the All-Father, who stood supported by his stout shield at the head of the army.

When the lines of nobles, princesses, druids, commanders, chieftains and warriors were finally assembled, the army of the Tuatha Dé Danann advanced across the plain of Moytura towards the oncoming Fir Bolg host.

As they came they beat their shields with swords, javelins and battle-axes and roared out their war cries across the plain. They filled the air with the wild wails of their war horns and the terrifying braying of leather-tongued battle-trumpets. Their marching feet raised huge dust clouds and through their ranks rushed the three terrible war-priestesses, the Badb, clad in their black robes and crimson veils, their hair dishevelled and brandishing in their hands dark-smoking torches.

Battalion after Battalion of the Tuatha Dé swept towards the Fir Bolg like great waves that crash on the echoing beach.

I, Tuan, was witness to all this. I heard the cries of the chieftains and saw the lines of shining, chequered warriors, fluttering with rich silken banners, turn and wheel beside the dark lakes and forests of the plain; their metalled war-shirts and bronze armour rippled like waves beneath the sun flooding the grasslands with gold.

From the east the Fir Bolg armies moved forward in silence, a brooding menacing host, roused to hatred of their enemy by the words of Fathach the poet.

As they advanced closer it seemed to the Fir Bolg that the hills around the plain had found a voice and taken up the Dé Danann war cry so great was the oncoming battle-clamour.

Now to the dismay of the Tuatha Dé a band of huge warriors, naked and painted for war, sprang from the ranks of the Fir Bolg, fearless hillmen howling like wolves for their prey.

The hearts of the Tuatha Dé were chilled for they knew now the fight would be a hard one and no easy victories could be won against such opponents.

Then in a single movement, four battle-groups separated from each army and faced each other.

With one will both sides advanced and the armies met at last with a clash of swords, spears and fighting men. The bosses of the shields met and a great roar went up.

3. THE BATTLE OF MOY TURA BEGINS.

I, Tuan, the sea-eagle, hovered over the field of battle, but the great dust cloud filled the golden circles of my eyes and I heard only the noise and tumult, the din and thunder, the loud striking of swords and the clangour of breast plates.

I heard the screams of the dying mixed with the vaunts of their destroyers.

Then, sinking lower through the battle-cloud I saw the pride and beauty of courage and youth made hideous by the slaughter of war. The earth ran with blood as the heads of men were hewn from their shoulders and bodies broken like splintered wood that kindles the fire of the hearth.

The wild hill-men of the Fir Bolg army were the first to kill that day when their chieftain, Nert Chu, slew Aidleo of the Tuatha Dé in single combat. The glued seams of their shields were torn from their fists so fierce was their fight; their swords were broken at the hilts and their spears wrenched from their rivets.

The Tuatha Dé held fast. Each warrior pressed on his neighbour with the edge of his shield, the shaft of his spear or the hilt of his sword so closely that they near wounded each other.

The naked Fir Bolg warriors were slowly forced back as the Dagda, followed by his bodyguard, cut a swathe through the ranks of the hillmen wide enough for one hundred and fifty men to follow towards the northern lakes.

At the same time Rua made a furious onslaught on the left flank of the Tuatha Dé and turned it. The heavy broad-pointed spears of the Fir Bolg pierced the unshielded sides of their enemies; fear spread like a forest fire through the Dé Danann ranks and their lines were broken. Yet in the midst of their terror they stood their ground even though they were surrounded by Rua and his brutal men of Miled, and everyone of them was cut down as the sharp edge of winter scythes the flowers of the field.

Like a wild tide Rua and the Fir Bolg army swept over the Dé Danann warriors until the ground was piled high with their dead and the earth slippery with the runnels of their blood. The Tuatha Dé Danann rearguard fought on bravely but by the close of day they were defeated and their lines scattered as they retreated towards their camp.

The Fir Bolg did not pursue them across the battlefield but returned in good spirits to their own camp. They each brought with them a stone and a severed head and placed them before Eochaí, the High King, until a great cairn was made of them.

Then Eochaí addressed his victorious host:

"Let this monument mark our victory and keep it alive for ever.

"Let it be the mark of our courage, for today we fought as fiercely as the wild boar who turns at bay with his back to the mountain and with one charge scatters the hounds and huntsmen who harass him.

"Let all men see this monument and long after the names of those who fought and lost are forgotten, let them remember our name, the name of the Fir Bolg, the name of the heroes who fought and won."

At the western side of the plain the Tuatha Dé raised a stone pillar, which was named the Pillar of Aidleo in tribute to the first of their brave soldiers who died. Nuada spoke to his men:

"We have been defeated today, but we fought valiantly and such a single defeat is no disgrace to a proud people like ours. Summon your courage, for now is the time for feats and daring, a time for heroes to show their powers and warcraft.

"Tomorrow we will triumph, have no fear, for they have used their strongest warriors today, while ours were kept in reserve. When the sun rises again we will drive through them as a scythe cuts through the fields, skimming the cornheads from the tall stalks."

Then Nuada summoned the physicians of the Tuatha Dé. They brought with them healing herbs and crushed and scattered them on the surface of the Well of Healing so that the precious waters became thick and green.

They carried their wounded to the Well and bathed them there until they were made whole again.

The Fir Bolg too practised their secret arts of healing, and so by the morrow those warriors who had survived on both sides were healed and refreshed.

4. THE STORY OF THE CHAMPIONS CAIRN

The next morning Eochaí, High King of the Fir Bolg went alone to the well to bathe before the day's battle.

As he bent over the water the bright reflection of the morning sun was blotted out by dark shadows. Turning, Eochaí saw three mysterious strangers standing shoulder to shoulder in all the splendour of their battle-array. With grim looks they summoned him to combat.

"I have come unarmed to bathe at the well," said the King, "Give me at least time to fetch my weapons."

"There can be no delay" said the strangers "for now is the time of the fight."

They moved with measured footsteps towards the unarmed king. Helpless as a child he stood.

Then the rays of the sun gathered before him like a shield and out of the brightness stepped a fourth warrior facing the three strangers.

"You will fight me and not the king" he said.

And so the four warriors fought together till each one of them was slain.

The Fir Bolg hearing the clash of weapons came running to the well. But the strangers were already laid out in the brotherhood of death. Eochaí bent over his unknown champion and his warm tears fell like rain on the cold face.

"Who is this handsome young hero who has laid down his life for me?" he asked.

But no one could answer his question.

Only I, Tuan, riding the high gold of morning, knew that Fate marks out inexorable patterns of time, and sends her own champions to marshall the true destinies of kings.

Yet still the Fir Bolg marvelled over the solitary stranger and to honour his bravery they each brought a white stone to the Well and piled a great cairn over his body.

It was called the Champions Cairn and stands fast even to this day.

PART FIVE

THE DREAM OF NUADA

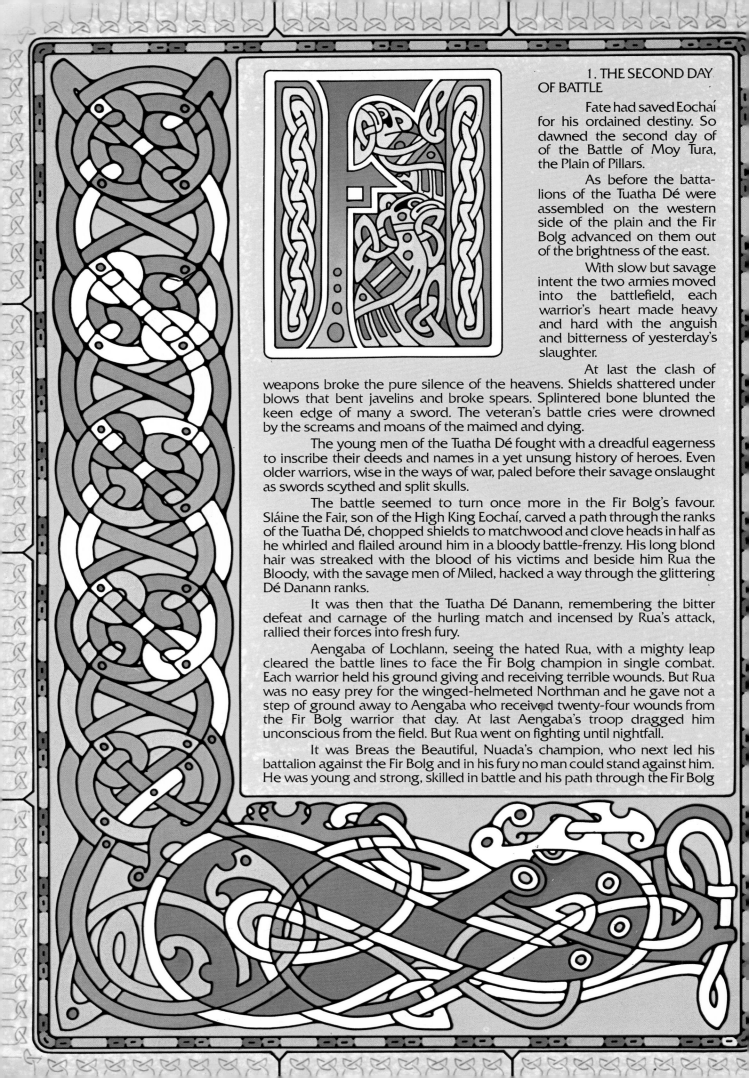

1. THE SECOND DAY OF BATTLE

Fate had saved Eochaí for his ordained destiny. So dawned the second day of of the Battle of Moy Tura, the Plain of Pillars.

As before the battalions of the Tuatha Dé were assembled on the western side of the plain and the Fir Bolg advanced on them out of the brightness of the east.

With slow but savage intent the two armies moved into the battlefield, each warrior's heart made heavy and hard with the anguish and bitterness of yesterday's slaughter.

At last the clash of weapons broke the pure silence of the heavens. Shields shattered under blows that bent javelins and broke spears. Splintered bone blunted the keen edge of many a sword. The veteran's battle cries were drowned by the screams and moans of the maimed and dying.

The young men of the Tuatha Dé fought with a dreadful eagerness to inscribe their deeds and names in a yet unsung history of heroes. Even older warriors, wise in the ways of war, paled before their savage onslaught as swords scythed and split skulls.

The battle seemed to turn once more in the Fir Bolg's favour. Sláine the Fair, son of the High King Eochaí, carved a path through the ranks of the Tuatha Dé, chopped shields to matchwood and clove heads in half as he whirled and flailed around him in a bloody battle-frenzy. His long blond hair was streaked with the blood of his victims and beside him Rua the Bloody, with the savage men of Miled, hacked a way through the glittering Dé Danann ranks.

It was then that the Tuatha Dé Danann, remembering the bitter defeat and carnage of the hurling match and incensed by Rua's attack, rallied their forces into fresh fury.

Aengaba of Lochlann, seeing the hated Rua, with a mighty leap cleared the battle lines to face the Fir Bolg champion in single combat. Each warrior held his ground giving and receiving terrible wounds. But Rua was no easy prey for the winged-helmeted Northman and he gave not a step of ground away to Aengaba who received twenty-four wounds from the Fir Bolg warrior that day. At last Aengaba's troop dragged him unconscious from the field. But Rua went on fighting until nightfall.

It was Breas the Beautiful, Nuada's champion, who next led his battalion against the Fir Bolg and in his fury no man could stand against him. He was young and strong, skilled in battle and his path through the Fir Bolg

line was marked by pools of blood.

Even though Rua made a fresh assault, it was in vain, and slowly the Fir Bolg were driven back towards their own camp. By nightfall they were defeated. But as before each warrior brought a stone and a head to add to the bloody cairn they were raising.

"Was it you, then, who were beaten today?" asked Eochaí as he embraced his battle-commanders returned from the field.

"Yes" said Rua.

"But it will not profit them" he added as he tossed his bloody trophy onto the gore-soaked cairn, where it lay face up, a soundless scream drawn on its mute lips.

I, Tuan, once a wild boar, now the sea eagle, had led my herds across this same plain following the scents of the turf and purple heather. Now I saw it transformed into a sad, spirit-haunted territory of pillars and cairns by that same force of history that had made me the winged bearer of myth.

By the night of that first day's fighting the dead were stripped and buried; where each hero fell a stone pillar was raised and around that pillar were set the cairns of the fallen warriors. It was a grim night's work and loud were the lamentations for loved ones slain that day.

2. THE THIRD DAY OF THE BATTLE

Next day was the third day of the First Battle of Moy Tura. This time it was the turn of Cirb, youthful champion, well-beloved of the Fir Bolg to try out his battle-valour for the first time. It was Cirb along with Streng and his two brothers who were to lead the Fir Bolg army this time.

They rose early in the morning and lined their forces across the plain, the four champions at the head of their battalions.

Protected by a solid wall of shields and a flashing forest of spears, the Fir Bolg moved forward towards the battle-line marked by the pillars on the plain; the great lowland which that day the Tuatha Dé Danann re-named Moy Tura, the Plain of Pillars, thus fulfilling the prophecy of Fathach. For, indeed, the whole field seemed like a forest of stone to those who gazed on it, so many were the pillars that caught the rays of the rising sun.

The Dagda led the Tuatha Dé Danann on that third day once again. He watched the silent Fir Bolg line approach his own.

"With vain pride and ceremony" he said "do the Fir Bolg assemble their battle-array. Those great war-groups might well strike fear into the hearts of poor mortal men. Yet they move like snails under their shield-shells and bristle like hedgehogs with their dazzling spear-spikes. But like the

hard-shelled snail and the sharp-spined hedgehog they have soft bellies under their armour and are mere flesh and blood for all their pomp and show. But today we have the advantage of them, for although they are led by a great man, you are led by a god."

Then the wide-waisted Dagda roared out his great laugh and led his sons, his brothers and all the Dé Danann kin across the field of Moy Tura, and set to smashing the armoured war groups, harrying the heavily armed hosts, disrupting their cunning formations, forcing them from their fixed positions around well-placed pillars and posts. For the Dagda had decided that his strategy would be first to smash the armoured shells of the Fir Bolg formations, and then to place each champion of his line against the stone pillars and wooden posts and have his warriors drive the enemy towards these positions.

Thus, with his back to the pillar each champion was safe from all except a strong forward thrust, for, with each blow the enemy ran the risk of a sword smashed on stone or embedded in wood, thus leaving themselves ripe for the death stroke.

The ferocious onslaught of the Dagda's four battalions forced the Fir Bolg from their stations, shattered their shields, burst their bosses from centre to rim and splintered their spears from shaft to spear head, twisting them back against the hands that held them.

Cirb, hearing the agonised cries of his warriors as they were driven towards the pillars and slaughtered, made a great charge from the east against the Dé Danann army. But Dagda in his turn heard the battling blows of Cirb as he cut his way through the contesting champions and turned to face the fierce Fir Bolg hero.

They sprang at each other as wild cats leap at their prey. Furious was the fight that followed, swift the shield-shattering strong blows.

Right through the long day they fought under the blaze of the merciless sun, which branded them with the heat of their armour. But at last Dagda found his mark and all the weight of the bronze of Cirb's crested war-helmet failed to stop the death-stroke which clove through metal, bone and brain and spilt the mortality of youth upon the thirsty ground.

Dagda lent panting on his sword; much of his fat flesh had melted in the heat of this fight and his sweat had mingled with his blood on the earth on which they had fought. But he felt small triumph, for there is little satisfaction in extinguishing the fire of youth when it blazes with such brilliance.

Even though Streng, their great war champion, sought to drive his men to great feats of bravery, the Fir Bolg were disheartened by Cirb's death and slowly fell back to their camp.

The Tuatha Dé did not pursue them but each man, following the fashion of the Fir Bolg, took a head and a stone pillar or post and carried them back to Nuada together with Cirb's head, which was set on top of the cairn known as the Cairn of Cirb's Head.

JIM FITZPATRICK

Anguish kept the Fir Bolg from rest that night and as for the Tuatha Dé, even their victory could not dispel their grief for the death of many of their finest young warriors who had fallen on that day and the two before.

The cost of the battle was great on both sides and the terrible cairns grew higher that night.

3. THE DREAM OF NUADA

I, Tuan, was sleepless too that night; crouched in my eyrie high above Belgatan my eyes pierced the dark.

I looked out towards the camp of the Tuatha Dé Danann and saw a huge raven drift across the night sky and alight on the blood-stained head of Cirb. Its wings shone blue-silver in the moonlight. Then it fluttered from its death-perch into the darkness and as I watched it vanish I saw a woman glimmering in the shade of Nuada's tent; a woman standing where the bird had gone.

She was Mórrigan, bearer of dreams that tangled in the darkness of her hair; dealer of death, war-witch blessed with beauty.

Beauty, death and dreams
are the substance of my myth.

So it was on the night of that third day of terrible battle that Mórrigan of the Badb put off her guises of witch and raven and stood a gentle maiden by Nuada's couch, her milk-white breasts scarce veiled by silks of saffron laced with gold.

"Come to me," he said. And she did. They lay long together that night wrapped in a cloak of darkness and the moon watched over them like the eye of the grey God of the Otherworld.

As they lay in the embrace of life, the moon gazed indifferently on the dead warriors locked in the embrace of death. Their arms had fallen across the still breasts of their fellows, hand touched hand; frozen gestures that mocked the brotherhood that had been forged in high heart and warm blood.

Nuada buried his face in the scent of Mórrigan's hair. The faces of the dead warriors were turned up towards the moon, some frozen in masks of horror, others made falsely young again, sleeping for ever like innocent children immune to harm or fearful dreams.

At last they slept and Nuada dreamed. But his dreams were troubled.

He saw mighty Empires rise and fall, the golden spires of legendary cities sink beneath raging seas and great armies move endlessly across barren continents.

His sleeping swept him back to the beginning of time far beyond memory and history. He walked with dreaming footsteps across the innocent brightness of a world remembered only in myth and legend; a

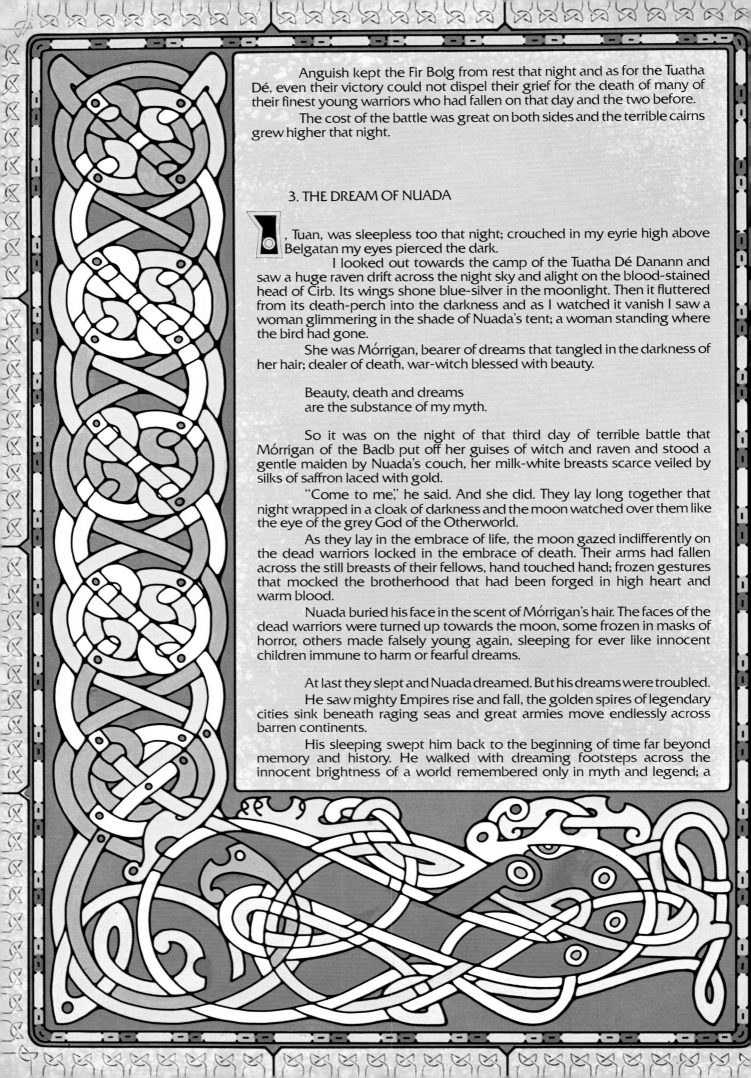

time when the Creator of men lived among his children and the sky was in the keeping of the Winged Warriors of the Dawn and the earth was ruled by beautiful bronze-skinned dragons who dwelt in palaces towering up into purple skies.

Then time turned like a fast-spinning wheel and Nuada saw the early beauty of the world broken by the pain and death of men whose lives were but a flicker in the eye of a god.

He saw the suffering of his forefathers, the race of Nemed, children of the Sun God. He saw Conann's Tower burn to the ground and the survivors flee from Éireann to the four corners of the earth. And in his dream Nuada, King of the Tuatha Dé Danann heard his own birth foretold and how he, Lord of Destiny, would lead the lost children of Nemed back to the sacred soil of Éireann, the Holy Ground.

But even as he heard himself named in his dream as the saviour of his people so Nuada saw a vision of his own tomorrow and his warriors slaughtered and piled dead on the blood-soaked plain of Moy Tura. He saw the cairns of severed heads that lay around each camp, and as his dream-self watched they opened staring, red-rimmed eyes and turning their white faces towards him with one voice they screamed:

"Enough."

"Enough," cried Nuada as he awoke, "the flooding streams of the blood of our dead will stain the green of this sacred soil for ever and make the teeming rivers and seas heavy and bitter with blood before we can call this land our own."

Yet even as his eyes pierced the darkness of dreaming Nuada saw the gold-bright beauty of Morrigan retreating from his arms, into the flickering shadows thrown by the burning tapers. There she settled in bird-shape and took the form of a raven once more. She spoke thus:

"O Nuada of the flaming hair,
restless you are this night.
Tomorrow you send your armies
to battle and certain slaughter.
The carrion of sons and kinsmen
will make fair feasting for ravens,
Birds of battle,
Birds of darkness
Birds of death."

But Nuada said:

"This carnage cannot be. We must use our sorcery to the full and stem the flood of death."

4. THE FOURTH DAY OF BATTLE

While Nuada had travelled the realms of myth and dark dreaming that third night, the sadness of Eochaí, High King of the Fir Bolg, had been lightened by the promise of mortal aid. From the distant hills of Corca Duibhue in Mumha, Fintan, his sons and his army of renowned warriors had come to join the Fir Bolg.

Thus the fourth morning of the Battle of Moy Tura found the Fir Bolg host in cheerful mood. The signals of the chieftains roused the fighting spirit in them and they began to hearten each other to meet danger and peril.

This time it was Eochaí, the High King, and his son Sláine the Fair who strode forth to lead the army of the Fir Bolg into battle.

They joined the centre with the Fir Bolg of Laighin, and the hosts of Cú Roi took the left flank, while the Fir Domhnann of Connacht took the right, with the army of the Galeoin drawn up in the rear. The thirteen sons of Fintan, warriors proven in battle, close-circled the person of Eochaí with a bristling wall of might that no enemy might breach and live to boast of.

So dawned the fourth and last day of the Battle of Moy Tura, a day of changing colours and fluctuating fortunes; of skilful and cunning weapon-play; a day of great courage and many terrible deaths.

The fighting was to be fierce; pitiless and terrible, hard-packed and close-knit; furious and far-flung; ebbing and flowing like the crested waves of a sea of adventure and peril.

I, Tuan, rode the high air above the battlefield. I saw the two armies meet in a great, rolling cloud of dust and heard the triumphant roars of heroes and champions mix with the cries of dying warriors.

5. THE DEATH-SONG OF FATHACH

The Fir Bolg advanced boldly to the firm-set pillars and batte-props set between them and the Tuatha Dé Danann. The Fir Bolg felt strong with the strength of mortal men.

But Nuada's dark dreaming had lent him the stored passion of myth and history. He knit his Dé Danann army together in tight patterns of wisdom and kinship. Grey-haired veterans used to the ways of battle were placed before fierce young warriors. The youthful fighters inexperienced, but brave, took their cue from the wiser men next to them. Older champions and faithful serving men were posted around and behind the flower of the Dé Danann youth for the king knew that no father would allow his son to be killed while a breath of life was left in his body.

Seers, sorcerers and wise men stood on the pillars and rocks round about, working strong magic and chanting incantations to their gods, while the poets and bards were to take count of the feats of bravery and compose them into song and written history.

The Fir Bolg were confident and brave. But the passionate Dé Danann atacked them furiously in close-knit companies fighting under the shelter of their speckled shields, bronze-bossed raven-emblazoned and spiral-marked.

As for Nuada himself, he was in the centre of the fight and strongly resolved to make short work of it. His princes and warriors were gathered round him, with the twelve sons of Gabhran from Scythia, his bodyguard, black-maned warriors of legendary courage.

They had set up their battle-props and pillars of rough-edged stone around their king and fastened their bodies to them with bands of leather and clasps of iron.

They knew that the Fir Bolg would soon try to dislodge them and that was their strategy.

While the battle raged Fathach, the poet of the Fir Bolg came to his own pillar and looking out on the armies surging from the East and West, sang his death-song:

"The host gather both power and might to meet on Moy Tura,
The speckled swords of the Fir Bolg resound
Against the graven shields of the Tuatha Dé
My race will lose many of their brothers
On this day.
Heads and severed limbs will litter the
Battle-ground.
Though the Fir Bolg will be cut down
Like corn in the field
Their death will be the harvest of keeness and valour.

"The Fir Bolg will be vanquished.
In death they will lie beside their broken blades
And split shields.
I will not put my trust in anyone
As long as I stay in stormy Éireann.

"I am Fathach the poet,
But grief has stopped the springs of my song
For death will sever the history of my race.
I too will yield up my body to the battle-fate
Of the Fir Bolg."

Fathach sang with the foresight of poet and seer, high on his pillar above the field. But below him the battle still raged in the balance of victory and the noise of it echoed across Moy Tura like the thunder that gathers in the storm clouds above Connacht.

PART SIX

THE BATTLE FRENZY
OF NUADA

s the battle blazed under the shimmering sun, Mórrigan, the crow of battle, came in the guise of a raven and alighted on the battle-pillar of Nuada.

As the fight neared the High King he began to put on his war-harness.

His white-tipped hair flowed like a bronze cloak from beneath his horned battle-helmet. Over his corded tunic of waxed double-skin, hard plated, lined with tanned leather strips, heat pressed, he fastened his twice-smelted, chain-link armour.

Then he buckled above him from waist to armpit, his battle-belt made of hard leather cut from the choicest parts of seven yearlings hides. Last of all he covered his chain armour with his apron of purple flax bordered with speckled gold, and painted his face with the signs of his race and rank.

Then he assembled his weapons: his rune-engraven sword with ivory hilt carved in the likeness of a man; nine small spears and nine sharp-pointed sleghs, nine darts, nine spikes and his clubs and battle-axes; his great round-shield so sharp-edged it could sever a man's head from his shoulders; his tall-standing feat-shield and his two curved skull-splitting Scythian swords.

When Nuada performed his long-shield leap-feat he could shear the locks of an enemy by leaping above the rim of his own shield, raising his powerful arms high, then bringing down his curved blade in a great arc on the naked neck of his enemy.

After he had dressed himself for battle Nuada turned to face Mórrigan, the golden-maid of his dreaming, now the dark, hunched crow of battle.

"Take your round raven-marked shield on your right arm" she said, "and cast it in the air after me." And with that she flew high above the Plain of Moy Tura.

With a great war-cry that echoed across the plain like the screams of a thousand warriors, Nuada hurled the shield after Mórrigan. And strangely the higher it went the bigger it grew until at last it blotted out the sun itself and turned day into night. And there it hung motionless.

To all who watched that day it seemed as if the shield was bigger than the sun itself. Even the Tuatha Dé who recognised the work of their own sorcerers were dismayed. But the unnatural darkness struck terror in the heart of the Fir Bolg warriors and made them easy prey for the Badb,

the three war-witches, who swooped down over their enemy with a phantom sky-born army of monsters, furies and hags.

Before them all, on chariots of fire, rode the Badb, those three war-witches Macha, Mórrigan and Nemaín. They rode above the darkened battlefield in a great circle, showering the Fir Bolg host with a rain of liquid fire from their blazing torches. Behind them the grotesque horrors they had conjured from the World of the Dead writhed across the sky.

Then with one voice they cried aloud. The sound echoed in the rocks and the waterfalls, and in all the hollows of the earth until it seemed that the whole world groaned its death-pang.

2. THE BATTLE FRENZY OF NUADA

t was then the first magical warp-spasm of battle-rage seized Nuada. His body shook and the earth beneath his feet trembled as he distorted his spirit-shape into that of a monstrous creature, hairy and voracious.

Poisonous mists spiralled around him and flames darted from his eyes. The hair rose up from his enormous head in a spiked and glowing halo piercing the darkness with all the colours of the earth.

Then Nuada, in his Sun God's terror and glory, called across the skies to the Riders of the Shí, the Faerie Host. And across the skies they came at his bidding, a crowd of wraith-like warriors, riding in terrible silence on winged horses.

Thus did Nuada, power-warped and filled with battle-fury, drive forward with his dark-maned Scythian body-guard among the trembling Fir Bolg and slay three hundred of them while their hands hung idle with fear.

Only Streng, that great champion of the Fir Bolg, stood firm against the onslaught of the Tuatha Dé Danann. Streng, wise to the ways of the Tuatha, had painted himself against such sorcery and wore three silver-disc talismans to ward off whatever magic the Dé Dananns could conjure that day. He alone stood against Nuada and his army determined not to flee until his battle-pillar should uproot itself and run.

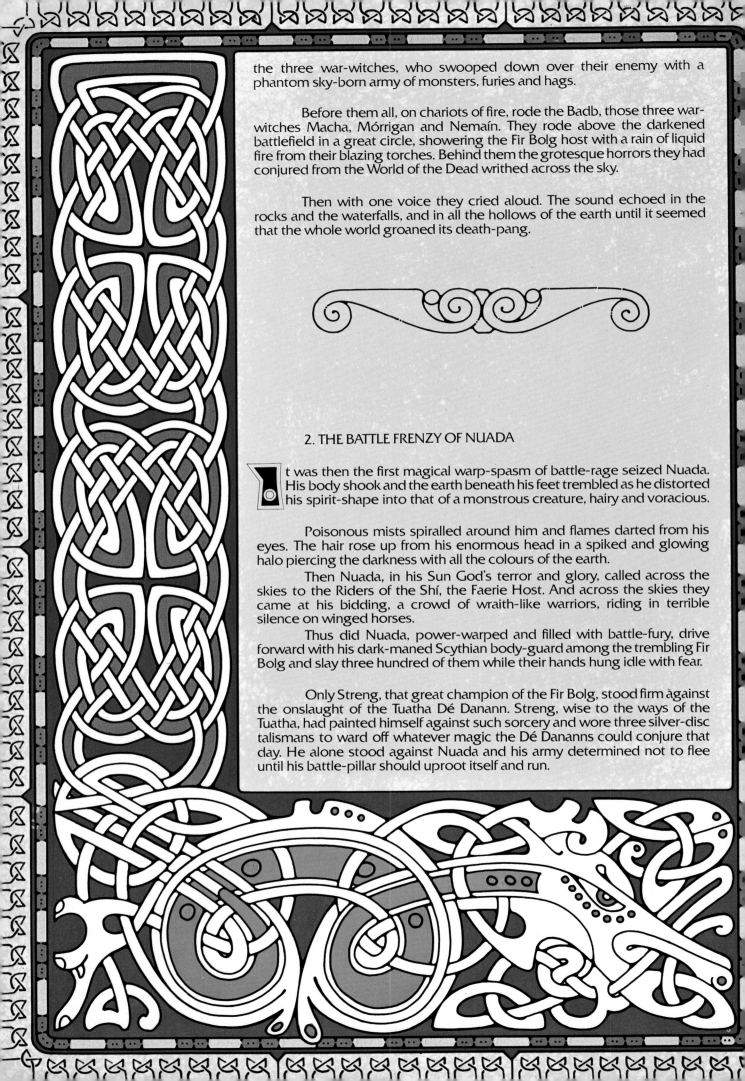

It was then that Breas the Beautiful, son of Éalathan the Immortal, and champion of the Tuatha Dé, made his onset on the Fir Bolg army and killed one hundred and fifty more of them.

He hacked arms, legs, and heads, from all who opposed him, as the huntsman carves and chops the raw flesh of his kill and cut a gorey path through the Fir Bolg of Laigin until he stood before Eochaí, the High King, and his bodyguard, the sons of Fintan. At a signal from the High King a path opened through his bodyguard, for Breas too, was of royal blood and lineage on his mother's side. Now he stood before Eochaí, who was glorious in his shining battle-array, and threw his sword into the ground before the High King of the Fir Bolg. With a stroke of his own longsword Eochaí lifted the challengers sword out of the turf and handed it back to him on the end of his blade. Breas struck nine blows on the long spiral-embossed shield of Eochaí and in return received nine blows from the king. With that Breas left Eochaí's position and took up the fight with his warriors.

Now Streng rallied his warriors and threw the Dé Dananns back to their own positions in a mighty counter-attack. Through the ranks of the Tuatha Dé he charged, and he carved a bloody way towards Nuada himself.

So it was that Breas found himself face to face with Streng but because of their Geassa, the bond of brotherhood they had made in the beginning when they had met outside the Dé Danann's first encampment, they did not fight.

Breas greeted Streng and then returned to his own side. But Streng continued his attack and though he left Breas untouched, he cut down all who opposed his drive for the Dé Danann centre leaving one hundred and fifty of the Tuatha Dé lying dead behind him.

Just as Eochaí, king of the Fir Bolg, had met Breas, champion of the Tuatha Dé Danann, in single combat, so now Nuada motioned aside his bodyguard and received in his turn nine blows from Streng, Champion of the Fir Bolg. But Streng had to bear in his turn nine wounds from the great ivory-hilted sword of Nuada before he withdrew to his own lines.

Still the battle raged. Strong spears were shattered by the death-pangs of warriors impaled on their points. Torn bodies hung from chipped pillars and splintered posts held fast by bloodstained thongs. Dis-emboweled bellies emptied entrails over gore-soaked grasslands.

The stench of death filled the evening air as the fight swung from one side of the battlefield to the other. Swords twisted and snapped against the hardened rims of bronze shields. Javelins and lances sang through the air. Many a brave and beautiful youth lay dead while blood and sweat dimmed the eyes of grey-haired veterans who waited for the call to arms.

I, Tuan, felt the anguish of that long day. I saw strongly tempered blades and vigorous young limbs break like brittle forest branches under the woodman's axe. Heroes swayed like tall grasses in the wind and fell as Death's harvest. Great was the glory, but terrible the bloodshed.

JIM FITZPATRICK

And still the killing continued through the supernatural darkness of that day.

3. THE SECOND FRENZY OF NUADA

Now despite the darkness that hung over them, the courage of the Fir Bolg grew as César, their druid, countered the sorcery of the Tuatha Dé Danann. Again César had called to the Great Worm, Crom-Crúach and again Crom-Crúach answered. Against the Badb and the wailing Riders of the Shí the demon worm-god sent the monstrous skeletal figure of the Collector of Lost Souls. Larger and larger it grew until it filled the sky and with a sweep of its bony fingers brushed the Riders of the Shí from the air around it. The horn-skulled demon quickly silenced the wailing that had so unnerved the Fir Bolg, then it turned to face those three war-witches, the Badb. Now the Badb had faced this great horned skeleton once before, in the time of Nemed himself, and knew that their magic was useless when pitted against the great power of this hideous emissary of the worm-god Crom-Crúach. Quickly the Badb returned to raven-form and sought sanctuary in the trees of the good earth.

Then the second mighty battle-frenzy shook Nuada and again the guise of the Sun-God was his. From the red jewel set in his horned helmet came a dazzling glow of living fire which pulsed and shimmered. In his hand the rune-engraven Claímh Solais, sword of light, turned from dull silver to blood-crimson till it, too, pulsed in time with the jewel. As the gigantic Collector turned to smite him Nuada called to his forefathers, then with an earth-shaking warcry he flung the burning sword of fire across the darkened sky and into the skull of the Collector.

With a shriek that froze all who heard it, the Collector faded back into the bowels of the earth and joined his fellow-fiends far from the sight of man.

I, Tuan, lord of the skies, soared high over Moy Tura to escape the horror of that dreadful spectre, whose fearful shrieking echoed across the darkened plain as it passed from the world of men into the world of demons and the damned.

Across the plain I flew, to the camp of the Fir Bolg where César, wizard-lord of legend, stood before his great ogham-carved pillar and chanted his spells. He had called to Crom-Crúach, and the Elder God, I knew, would soon seek reward for his services.

Lebor Gabála

PART SEVEN

THE LAST BATTLE AND
THE DEATH OF EOCHAÍ

1. THE DEATH OF CÉSAR.

Now the cold sweat of fear darkened César's white hair. The penalty of failure was his, a hideous price beyond imagination. He had spoken words forbidden him by all the laws of his race; invocations from the primitive and savage past. He had called upon Crom-Crúach the primeval god whose name should not be spoken. He had prayed that he should stay the power of the Dé Danann sorcery, but he had perverted the divine order of the otherworld. The wrath he had to face now was not the wrath of mortal men, the anger of his fellow-druids, nor even of the High King, but the rage of the Worm God. For the Elder-Gods do not intervene in the affairs of men without payment and in return for his divine intercession Crom-Crúach had demanded a terrible reward: he had craved the souls of slain heroes. But when he sent his Collector he had been blocked by the superior magic of the sorcerers of the Tuatha Dé Danann, the druids of Nuada, child of the Sun-God. Crom-Crúach writhed in an agony of humiliation; he would not wait long for vengeance, nor would he be denied his grisly feasting.

Now in his terror César called on the new gods to save him. His heart brittle with fear the Fir Bolg druid grovelled before that same magical stone pillar he had carved and planted with high hope before the battle. The gods were silent but great storm clouds gathered above him blotting out the sun again and César knew that all was lost. In his panic he turned to flee but the magic circle he had chalked held him. He cried to the heavens which mocked him with a dead echo of his fear. The new gods would not heed the prayers of a faithless man, however skilled in sorcery.

A green glow outlined the pillar against the darkness and the shadows twisted themselves in a great hand, powerful, almost invisible, which caught César and forced him down again before the great pillar. In his anguish he screamed to the demon-lord, but the ghost-clutch only grew stronger. The ghastly fire burned brighter and slime ran down the ogham-carved pillar and slowly engulfed César, melting and devouring his quivering flesh with a sound of obscene and greedy sucking. The Fir Bolg people watched horror-stricken as their wizard shuddered away his life in a dumb agony of horror.

I, Tuan, flew up and away from César's terrible monument. I lamented his passing, for he was not an evil man only misguided by love and

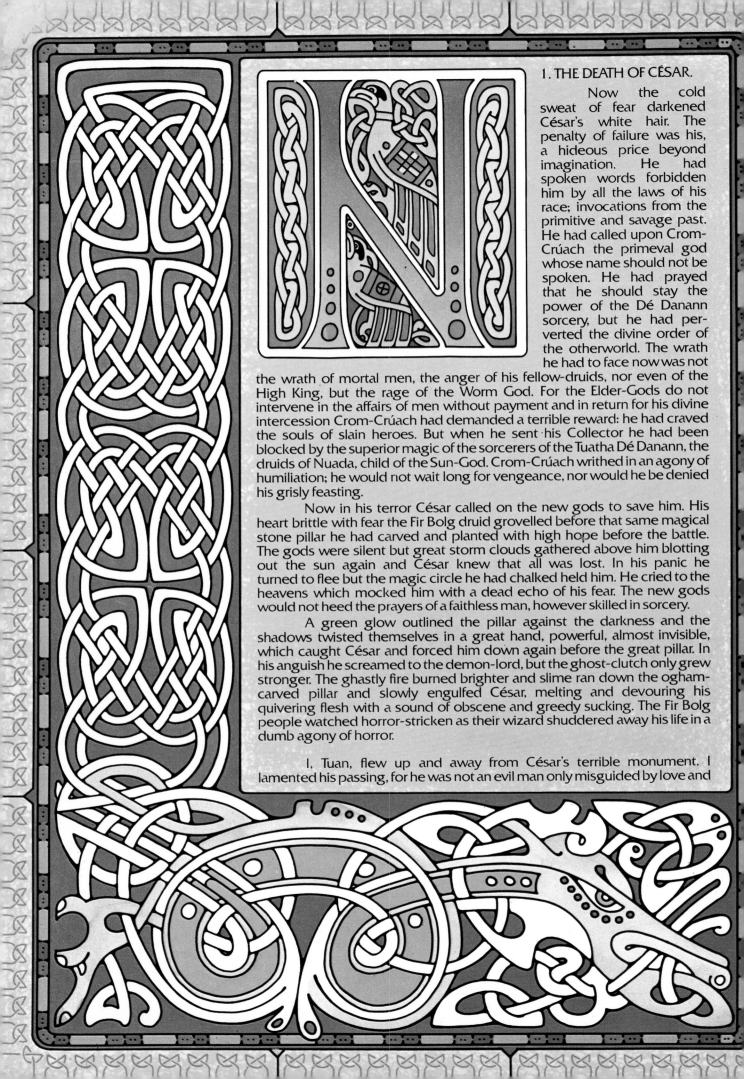

JIM FITZPATRICK

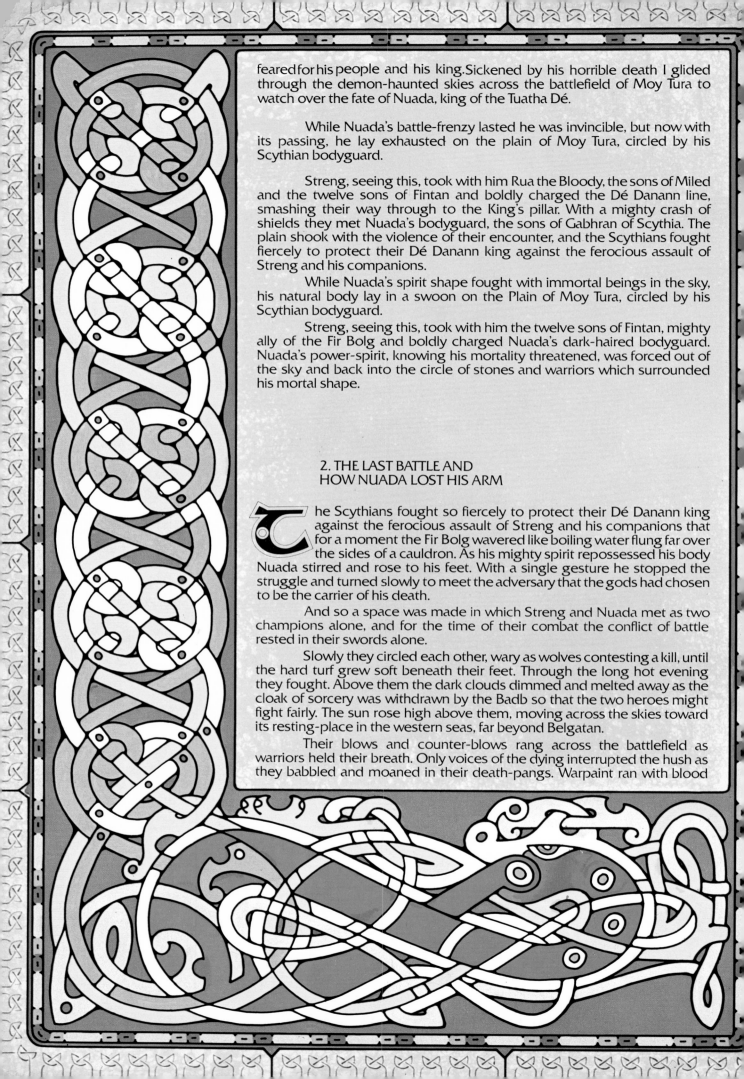

feared for his people and his king. Sickened by his horrible death I glided through the demon-haunted skies across the battlefield of Moy Tura to watch over the fate of Nuada, king of the Tuatha Dé.

While Nuada's battle-frenzy lasted he was invincible, but now with its passing, he lay exhausted on the plain of Moy Tura, circled by his Scythian bodyguard.

Streng, seeing this, took with him Rua the Bloody, the sons of Miled and the twelve sons of Fintan and boldly charged the Dé Danann line, smashing their way through to the King's pillar. With a mighty crash of shields they met Nuada's bodyguard, the sons of Gabhran of Scythia. The plain shook with the violence of their encounter, and the Scythians fought fiercely to protect their Dé Danann king against the ferocious assault of Streng and his companions.

While Nuada's spirit shape fought with immortal beings in the sky, his natural body lay in a swoon on the Plain of Moy Tura, circled by his Scythian bodyguard.

Streng, seeing this, took with him the twelve sons of Fintan, mighty ally of the Fir Bolg and boldly charged Nuada's dark-haired bodyguard. Nuada's power-spirit, knowing his mortality threatened, was forced out of the sky and back into the circle of stones and warriors which surrounded his mortal shape.

2. THE LAST BATTLE AND HOW NUADA LOST HIS ARM

The Scythians fought so fiercely to protect their Dé Danann king against the ferocious assault of Streng and his companions that for a moment the Fir Bolg wavered like boiling water flung far over the sides of a cauldron. As his mighty spirit repossessed his body Nuada stirred and rose to his feet. With a single gesture he stopped the struggle and turned slowly to meet the adversary that the gods had chosen to be the carrier of his death.

And so a space was made in which Streng and Nuada met as two champions alone, and for the time of their combat the conflict of battle rested in their swords alone.

Slowly they circled each other, wary as wolves contesting a kill, until the hard turf grew soft beneath their feet. Through the long hot evening they fought. Above them the dark clouds dimmed and melted away as the cloak of sorcery was withdrawn by the Badb so that the two heroes might fight fairly. The sun rose high above them, moving across the skies toward its resting-place in the western seas, far beyond Belgatan.

Their blows and counter-blows rang across the battlefield as warriors held their breath. Only voices of the dying interrupted the hush as they babbled and moaned in their death-pangs. Warpaint ran with blood and sweat and the two heroes cut and thrust at each other. Clubs, battle-axes, spears, spikes and darts crashed against strong shields, tough hides, firm chain-mail and soft flesh. Each one inflicted thirty wounds upon the other until at last Nuada, weakened by the exertion of his magic, fell against his pillar. The Scythian guards tied him upright with leather thongs then with one last defiant warcry he struck a great blow on Streng's long, spiral-patterned war-shield. But in return Streng dealt a mighty sword-thrust downward past the pillar's edge, which, cutting through the rim of Nuada's shield, struck his right arm cleaving flesh and bone, making the Dé Danann king defenceless as an untrained youth.

It was then, while Nuada lay helpless on the bloodstained battlefield, that Aengaba of Lochlann entered the fray to protect him. With his winged helmet and shining chain-mail singlet, he was a handsome hero but soon his good looks were stained with his own blood, as he turned his weapons furiously against Streng. With his first sword-blow he struck Streng's horned war-helmet from his head. They fought long and fiercely but Streng's broad blade and sharp battle-axe dealt deeper, deadlier wounds. As soon as the Dagda heard the music of swords in battle-stress he came to the place of conflict with great bounds, like the rush of a mighty waterfall.

But Streng refused to fight two champions. Even so though Aengaba of Lochlann, Lord of the frozen Northlands, did not fall there, it was from the violence of Streng's sword thrusts that he afterwards died.

The Dagda stood over Nuada, his king and after the Tuatha Dé had taken council, he brought fifty soldiers with their physicians and they carried their wounded king from the field, and the fighting was resumed.

3. THE DEATH OF EOCHAÍ

The Tuatha Dé were not stayed in their keen fighting by their king's misfortune and Breas the Beautiful and his warriors forced their way through the ranks of the Fir Bolg in a desperate effort to avenge their king, Nuada. They hacked a path through to where Eochaí, High King of the Fir Bolg was urging the battle, exhorting his heroes and arranging his combats.

Savage was the fight that followed and Breas was so badly wounded by Eochaí that he had to be dragged from the battlefield by his bodyguard.

Even so, the hour of the Fir Bolg had come. The sands of time had run out for them and I, Tuan, sea eagle, knew that fate had decreed that victory was not to be theirs for all their bravery.

The tiring hosts of the Fir Bolg were driven back by the Dé Danann attacks led by the mighty Dagda. Their faltering ranks held, then broke, and warriors once valiant fled like hares before a grassfire.

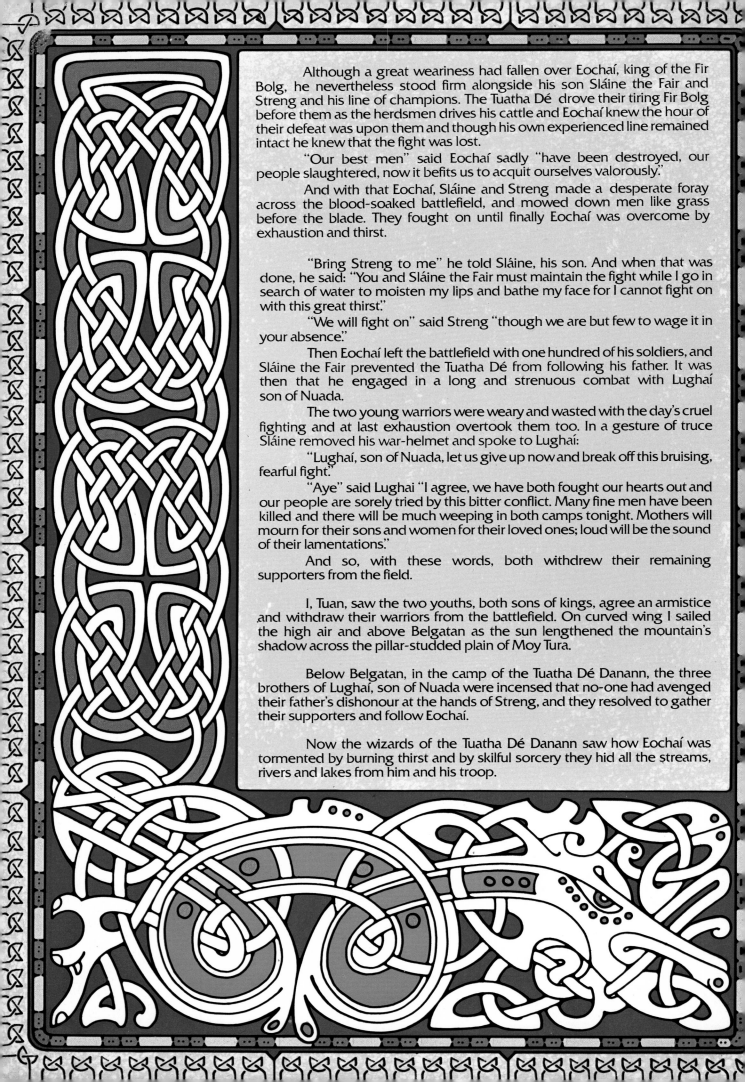

Although a great weariness had fallen over Eochaí, king of the Fir Bolg, he nevertheless stood firm alongside his son Sláine the Fair and Streng and his line of champions. The Tuatha Dé drove their tiring Fir Bolg before them as the herdsmen drives his cattle and Eochaí knew the hour of their defeat was upon them and though his own experienced line remained intact he knew that the fight was lost.

"Our best men" said Eochaí sadly "have been destroyed, our people slaughtered, now it befits us to acquit ourselves valorously."

And with that Eochaí, Sláine and Streng made a desperate foray across the blood-soaked battlefield, and mowed down men like grass before the blade. They fought on until finally Eochaí was overcome by exhaustion and thirst.

"Bring Streng to me" he told Sláine, his son. And when that was done, he said: "You and Sláine the Fair must maintain the fight while I go in search of water to moisten my lips and bathe my face for I cannot fight on with this great thirst."

"We will fight on" said Streng "though we are but few to wage it in your absence."

Then Eochaí left the battlefield with one hundred of his soldiers, and Sláine the Fair prevented the Tuatha Dé from following his father. It was then that he engaged in a long and strenuous combat with Lughaí son of Nuada.

The two young warriors were weary and wasted with the day's cruel fighting and at last exhaustion overtook them too. In a gesture of truce Sláine removed his war-helmet and spoke to Lughaí:

"Lughaí, son of Nuada, let us give up now and break off this bruising, fearful fight."

"Aye" said Lughai "I agree, we have both fought our hearts out and our people are sorely tried by this bitter conflict. Many fine men have been killed and there will be much weeping in both camps tonight. Mothers will mourn for their sons and women for their loved ones; loud will be the sound of their lamentations."

And so, with these words, both withdrew their remaining supporters from the field.

I, Tuan, saw the two youths, both sons of kings, agree an armistice and withdraw their warriors from the battlefield. On curved wing I sailed the high air and above Belgatan as the sun lengthened the mountain's shadow across the pillar-studded plain of Moy Tura.

Below Belgatan, in the camp of the Tuatha Dé Danann, the three brothers of Lughaí, son of Nuada were incensed that no-one had avenged their father's dishonour at the hands of Streng, and they resolved to gather their supporters and follow Eochaí.

Now the wizards of the Tuatha Dé Danann saw how Eochaí was tormented by burning thirst and by skilful sorcery they hid all the streams, rivers and lakes from him and his troop.

One hundred and fifty of the Dé Danann reserve led by the three brothers of Lughaí, son of Nuada, hunted the Fir Bolg down until they confronted him by the strand of Eochaill. There the two armies engaged in bloody battle. The three sons of Nuada were fiercely intent on revenging their father and venomous was their attack on Eochaí's weary war-party. Great numbers fell on both sides, but the Dé Dananns were the fresher and held the upper hand.

Eochaí was well used to fighting against great odds and his last irresistible onset against the warriors of the Tuatha Dé was like the sudden brilliance of a shooting star which tears a fiery path across the nightsky before it passes into the oblivion of darkness.

This was his last fight and his most heroic one. With a great cry he swept the enemy before him and slew many a younger man, and drove the three sons of Nuada into the sea. With the fish running before them they hacked and cut each other with clubs, sword, spears and knives until the white-foam waves were stained with their blood.

Like the battle-hardened veteran he was, Eochaí battered and smashed the shields of the sons of Nuada and hacked and scarred their unprotected flesh.

Before he fell, his body torn and his chest cut open by savage sword strokes, he slew all three of the young sons of Nuada in his last great death-duel.

Where he fell, he was buried, and his cairn is called Cairn Eochaí. The gravestones of the three Dé Dananns are at the western end of the strand, and all are there to this day.

I, Tuan, mourned the passing of Eochaí, for he was a just and noble king, the first in Éireann to be called Árd-Dí, that is High King. But Fate was not on his side; the coming of the Tuatha Dé Danann and their conquest of the island had spelt disaster for Eochaí and the Fir Bolg.

As for Streng, the greatest of the heroes, he continued fighting for a day and a night after his people had given up the fight. At last, he too yielded to exhaustion.

By now neither side had strength enough to attack the other. Their sword arms had grown weak with slaughter, their spirits were low because of their wounds, and their courage was faint because of the great disasters that had befallen them, the loss of beloved sons, brothers, fathers and kinsmen.

So they departed from the Plain of Pillars; the Fir Bolg returning to their camp in the east and the Tuatha Dé retiring to their fortress below Belgatan. Now the blood-soaked Plain of Moy Tura was left empty and Dagda looked over the battle-pillars and cairns of dead and spoke these words:

"Soldiers have been slain beyond number
Many the wounds endured by great heroes
Cruel swords have torn away beauty from bodies
Terrible are the losses of battle.

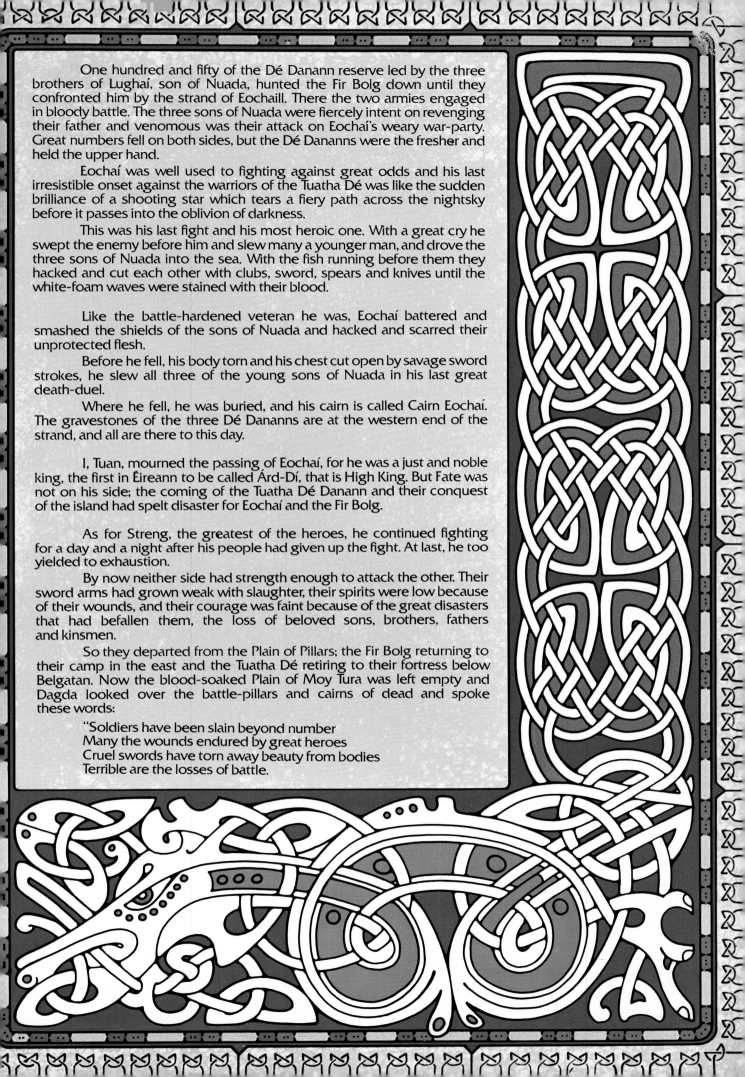

JIM FITZPATRICK

"It was Streng who was the greatest hero
Though our host won the battle
For our king Nuada lost his arm
But brave King Éochaí lost his head.

"Only now have we at last come home
Back to the land of our fathers, sons of Nemed.
After battle we may sow the seeds of peace
And reap a golden harvest from this fertile soil.

"Our sons will inherit the cloud-topped mountains,
They will build dwellings fit for children of heroes,
And mothers will rock gold-studded cradles
And lull babies asleep with sung-stories of heroes."

Then he raised his sword to the sky and chanted:

"Decisive days
Auspicious hours
We witness
Slaughtered soldiers;
Wounded warriors
We behold.

Fertile fields
Abundant rivers
We inherit."

4. STRENG SPARES NUADA

The people of the Fir Bolg were sad and weary that night. Each one stripped and buried sons and brothers, kinsmen and friends. Mounds were raised over brave men; cairns over warriors and hills over heroes.

After that was done, Streng and his brothers called a meeting and assembled three hundred fighting men to consider what should be done; whether they should leave Éireann, offer further battle or share the land with the Tuatha Dé Danann. The Assembly decided to offer the Dé Dananns battle but Streng was against this and said:

"Resistance means destruction and the death of more of our fine warriors. The battle was a fair and brave one, we fought with strength and resolution. There was clashing of strong swords, hard plying of spears, great valour and great slaughter.

"There has been too much sadness and bloodshed on the green plains of Éireann, death and disaster in its dappled woodlands. Too many good men have been lost. Let us find some peaceful solution after so much suffering and grief."

But the Fir Bolg warriors would not listen to Streng's wise words and they voted once more for battle. The three hundred again took up their strong hooked shields, their venomous spears and their sharp blue-bladed swords.

They made a last ferocious charge across the battlefield to the Dé Danann fort and cut their way through the gates. They were a wild and fiery war group carving their way through the unprepared warriors of the Tuatha Dé in a fury of revenge, unafraid of pain or death.

It was then that Streng, who had led that last final onslaught against his will, challenged Nuada to single combat, to complete the fight they had began in the previous battle.

Nuada, though sorely injured and pained by the loss of his strong right arm, faced Streng bravely as if he had been whole and resisting the offers of others to fight in his stead spoke out firmly:

"If it is single combat on fair terms you seek, then you must fasten up your right hand, for I have lost mine."

"If you have lost your hand" said Streng, "then there is no obligation to fight, for our first combat was an equal one on equal terms. The fight was ours alone and has been resolved."

With this magnanimous gesture Streng spared Nuada death and defeat. After declaring truce the Tuatha Dé took council and at the urging of Nuada and Breas agreed to offer Streng a choice of the provinces of Éireann, and decided that a pact of peace, goodwill and friendship should be made between their two peoples.

Streng agreed to this and after deliberation, his assembly chose the land of Connacht for the Fir Bolg, Fir Domhnann and Galeoin, while the people of Cú Roi were allowed return to their northern homeland unhindered.

Thus did Streng and his people take possession of the province of Connacht, a dwelling place bought dearly from the Tuatha Dé Danann with the blood of brave warriors and thus did the Tuatha Dé Danann take the land of Éireann from the Fir Bolg.

And that is the story of the First Battle of Moy Tura, the Plain of Pillars, and the Conquest of the Tuatha Dé Danann.

"It would have been wiser to have given them the half of Éireann in the first place," Streng was heard to say long after, "for we gained nothing in the fighting but lost almost everything."

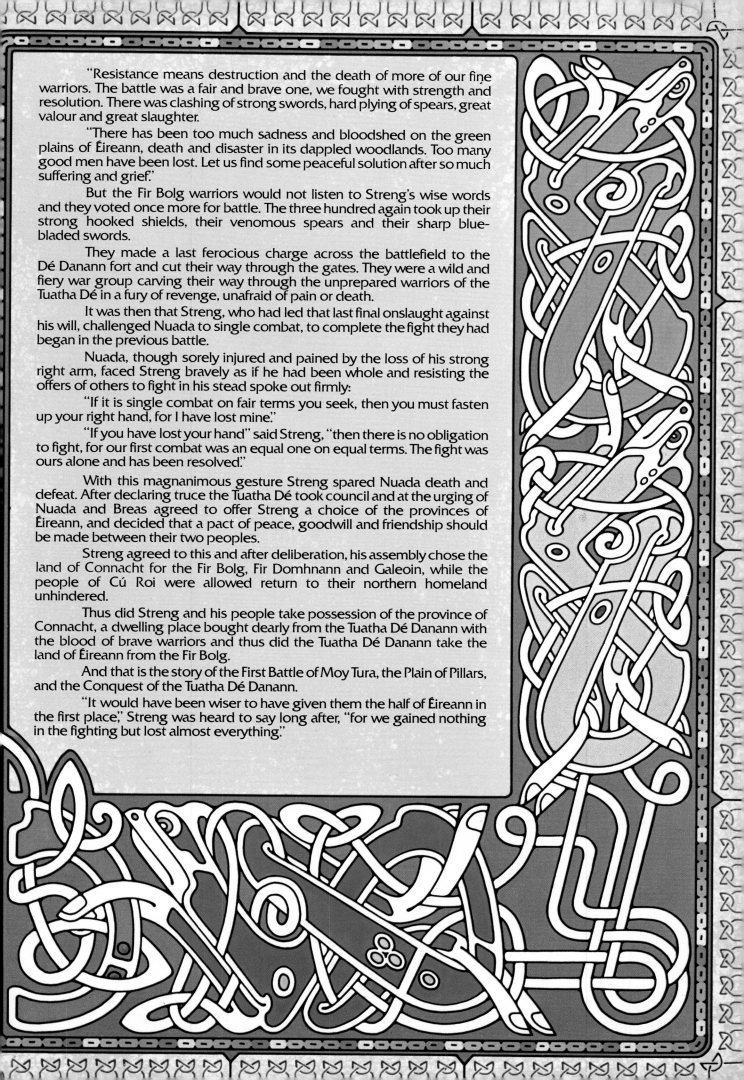

EPILOGUE

After the First Battle of Moy Tura, the Tuatha Dé Danann made Breas the Beautiful their king, for although Nuada had led them to Éireann and won the battle for them, it was their law and custom that no man that was not perfect in shape should be king and their laws could never be broken.

But the rule of Breas, son of Eolatan the Immortal of the Fomor, was an oppressive one and the proud Dé Danann were forced to pay tribute to Balor of the Evil Eye, King of the Fomor. In the meantime Nuada had been fitted by Dian-Cecht, the healer, with an arm of silver miraculously made so that each joint answered his will as though it was his own flesh and blood.

He was reinstated in the sovereignity by his people and from that time forth known as Nuada Airgitlámh, that is, Nuada of the Silver Arm, and his name is remembered to this day in the myths and legends of his people.

He was slain by Balor of the Evil Eye in the Second Battle of Moy Tura, though Balor too was killed by the greatest hero of the Tuatha Dé Danann, Lugh Samildanach. The evil Fomor were finally routed in that battle and expelled forever from the land and seas of Éireann.

I, Tuan, sea-eagle, witnessed all these great events through my many lives and remembered them through many centuries until I was made man again and born as Tuan son of Carill, King of Ireland.

In my old age I told my story to the priest Finnian of the Church of the Bells. It is he and his scribes who preserved it for eternity.   .

These pages are no poet's dreamings or madman's musings; they are more than half-shaped memories wrested from the oblivion of time; they are the true histories of heroes and long dead races. This is their story and mine.

I am memory turned myth.

I am legend.

I am Tuan.

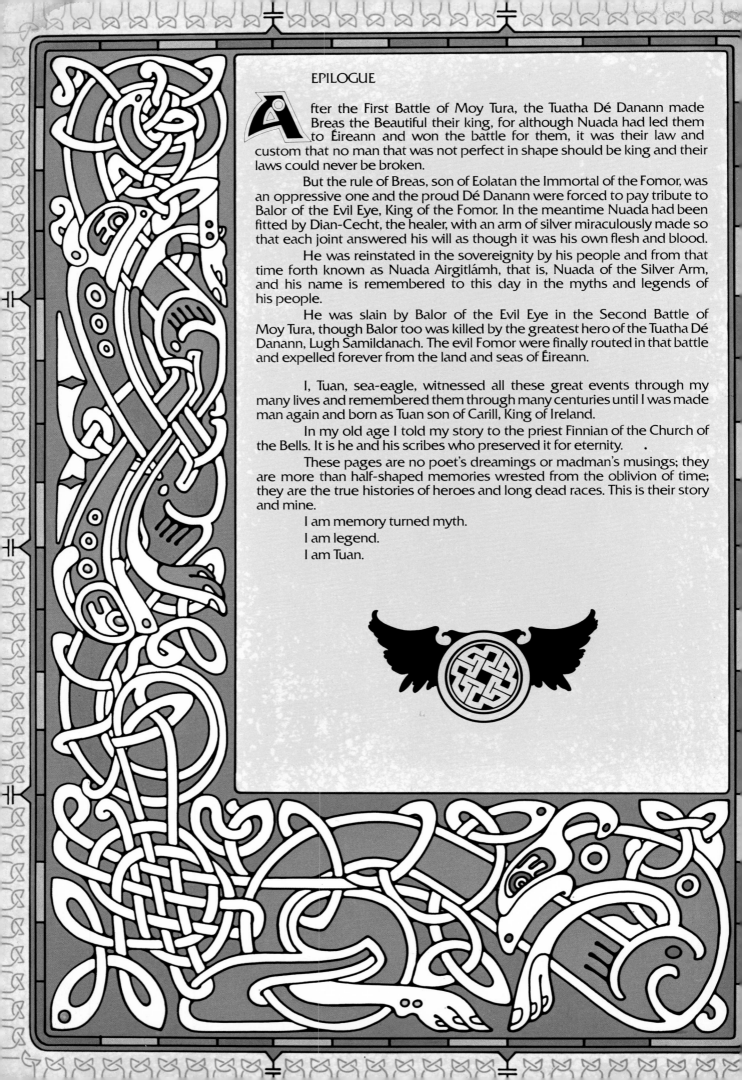

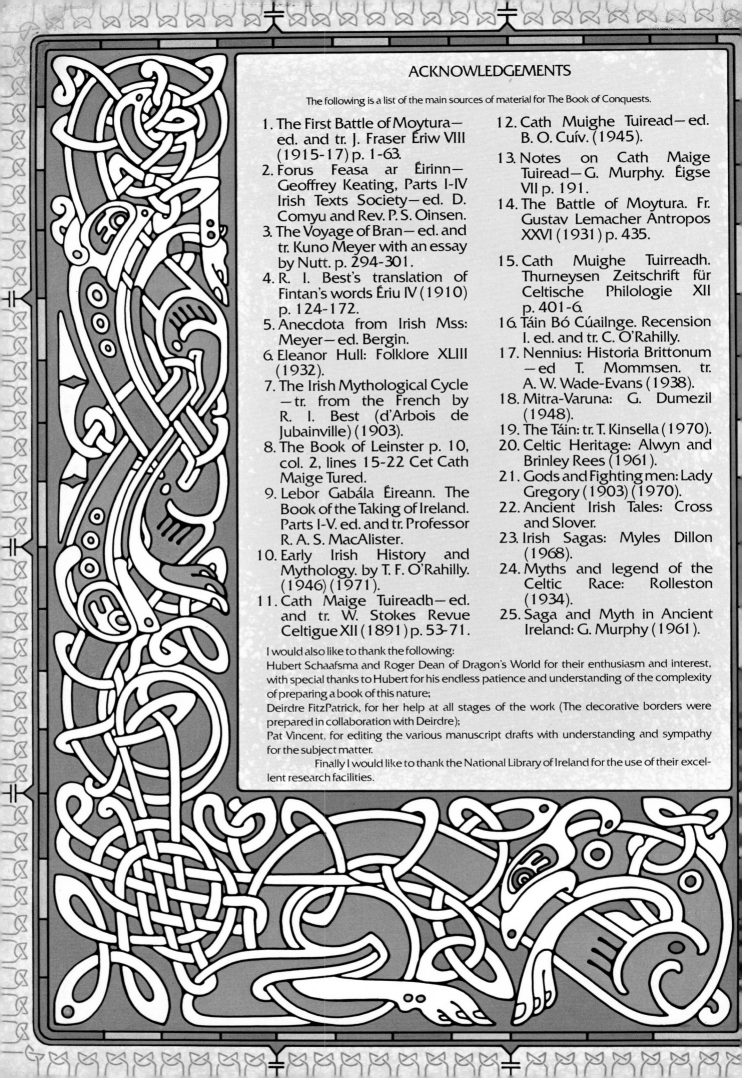

ACKNOWLEDGEMENTS

The following is a list of the main sources of material for The Book of Conquests.

1. The First Battle of Moytura— ed. and tr. J. Fraser Ériw VIII (1915-17) p. 1-63.

2. Forus Feasa ar Éirinn— Geoffrey Keating, Parts I-IV Irish Texts Society— ed. D. Comyu and Rev. P. S. Oinsen.

3. The Voyage of Bran— ed. and tr. Kuno Meyer with an essay by Nutt. p. 294-301.

4. R. I. Best's translation of Fintan's words Ériu IV (1910) p. 124-172.

5. Anecdota from Irish Mss: Meyer— ed. Bergin.

6. Eleanor Hull: Folklore XLIII (1932).

7. The Irish Mythological Cycle — tr. from the French by R. I. Best (d'Arbois de Jubainville) (1903).

8. The Book of Leinster p. 10, col. 2, lines 15-22 Cet Cath Maige Tured.

9. Lebor Gabála Éireann. The Book of the Taking of Ireland. Parts I-V. ed. and tr. Professor R. A. S. MacAlister.

10. Early Irish History and Mythology. by T. F. O'Rahilly. (1946) (1971).

11. Cath Maige Tuireadh— ed. and tr. W. Stokes Revue Celtigue XII (1891) p. 53-71.

12. Cath Muighe Tuiread— ed. B. O. Cuív. (1945).

13. Notes on Cath Maige Tuiread— G. Murphy. Éigse VII p. 191.

14. The Battle of Moytura. Fr. Gustav Lemacher Antropos XXVI (1931) p. 435.

15. Cath Muighe Tuirreadh. Thurneysen Zeitschrift für Celtische Philologie XII p. 401-6.

16. Táin Bó Cúailnge. Recension I. ed. and tr. C. O'Rahilly.

17. Nennius: Historia Brittonum — ed T. Mommsen. tr. A. W. Wade-Evans (1938).

18. Mitra-Varuna: G. Dumezil (1948).

19. The Táin: tr. T. Kinsella (1970).

20. Celtic Heritage: Alwyn and Brinley Rees (1961).

21. Gods and Fighting men: Lady Gregory (1903) (1970).

22. Ancient Irish Tales: Cross and Slover.

23. Irish Sagas: Myles Dillon (1968).

24. Myths and legend of the Celtic Race: Rolleston (1934).

25. Saga and Myth in Ancient Ireland: G. Murphy (1961).

I would also like to thank the following:

Hubert Schaafsma and Roger Dean of Dragon's World for their enthusiasm and interest, with special thanks to Hubert for his endless patience and understanding of the complexity of preparing a book of this nature;

Deirdre FitzPatrick, for her help at all stages of the work (The decorative borders were prepared in collaboration with Deirdre);

Pat Vincent, for editing the various manuscript drafts with understanding and sympathy for the subject matter.

Finally I would like to thank the National Library of Ireland for the use of their excellent research facilities.